# From Jerusalem to Jericho

# Other Works by Al Hill

## Our Evil—God's Good
*And Other Sermons from Genesis through Joshua*

## Things That Kings Can't Do
*And Other Sermons*
*from Judges through 2nd Kings, and the Wisdom Books*

## In the Presence of the Lord
*And Other Sermons from the Psalms and the Prophets*

## Walking with Jesus
*And Other Sermons from the Gospel of Matthew*

## God's Purpose for Your Faith
*And Other Sermons from Mark, Hebrews, James and 1st Peter*

## Traits of the Shepherd
*And Other Sermons from the Gospel of John, 1st John and Revelation*

## Making Peace with Your Father
*And Other Sermons from Paul's Letters to the Romans and Corinthians*

## The Empty God
*And Other Sermons from the Shorter Letters of Paul*

## O Come, Let God Adore Us
*And Other Sermons for Advent and Christmas*

## Not Exactly What They Expected
*And Other Sermons for Holy Week and Easter*

## DEAR TRINITY
Letters from a Pastor to His People

# From Jerusalem to Jericho

*And Other Sermons*
*from the Gospel of Luke and the Acts of the Apostles*

## Al Hill

SOMMERTON
HOUSE

Copyright © 2018 Al Hill

Because of the dynamic nature of the Internet, any web addresses or links contained in this book may have changed since publication and may no longer be valid.

Cover design by the author.

The image on the cover depicting The Good Samaritan is from a stained-glass window located in New St. James Presbyterian Church, London, Ontario, Canada. The image is used with the kind permission of the Church Session.

ISBN: 978-1-948773-20-1 (sc)

Library of Congress Control Number: 2018906515

To learn more about, or to purchase, this or other works by Al Hill, go to www.sommertonhouse.com
or amazon.com/author/alhill

*Dedication*

To my brother, Lewis,

who has taught me more
about courage, kindness and character—
all by his quiet example—
than anyone else I know.

# Contents

## Sermons

### From the Gospel of Luke

## From the Acts of the Apostles

## Indices

# Preface

*"A man was going down from Jerusalem to Jericho...."*

*"There was a man who had two sons...."*

*"Two men went up to the temple to pray...."*

*"The land of a rich man produced plentifully...."*

*"A man once gave a great banquet and invited many...."*

*"There was a rich man who was clothed in purple and fine linen...."*

৵৽৽

Jesus told stories about people—some ordinary, some anything but—to tell people the extraordinary story of God's salvation, now available to them in the Person of One Who looked for all the world to be just like one of them. The stories Jesus told are found in all four Gospels, but some of the most memorable, and powerful, are found in Luke alone.

Jesus created a world with words that seems very much like the world created with divine words "in the beginning"—the world the people who listened to His stories knew so well. But the "story world" of Jesus turned out to be very different from what people had come to expect in their world. His stories revealed a world unexpectedly different from, and far better than, the one they knew.

Jesus had come not just to tell them about this other and better world, but to take them to it. But before people could go there, they had to realize there was a different world to go to. And then they had to learn what was required of them to get there. And for this, Jesus told them stories.

Relating the parables of Jesus was not all Luke did in his Gospel, and his Gospel was not all he wrote to present the story of Jesus—from His miraculous birth through His earthly ministry to His death and resurrection—and beyond. Luke told the *stories* of Jesus as part of the *story* of Jesus (in the Gospel) and of His Church (in the Acts of the Apostles). The *stories* of Jesus continue to be told today—and the *story* continues to be written, in our lives and the lives of hundreds of millions of other people who have heard what Jesus said and have seen the other world His words revealed. Every day, people go down the road from Jerusalem to Jericho with Jesus—and find themselves in a far better world as a result.

ॐ

*From Jerusalem to Jericho* is a collection of 32 sermons based on texts from the Gospel of Luke and the Acts of the Apostles. The sermons were written over a number of years and were preached in various Navy chapels and civilian churches.

During many of those years, I used the Revised Common Lectionary to select the texts for the sermons. The three-year repeating cycle provided multiple opportunities to preach from the same passages. As a result, you will find two sermons in the pages that follow dealing with the wilderness temptation of Jesus, two treatments of the dinner Jesus attended at Simon the Pharisee's house, two sermons about the Good Samaritan, and three growing out of Jesus' encounter with Zacchaeus.

In almost all cases, the sermons in this book were preached under rigid time constraints, either because there were multiple services scheduled for Sunday morning or because the sermons were being broadcast on the radio. The maximum time available for the sermon in these circumstances was generally 18 minutes. The even shorter homilies among the sermons were delivered at early morning communion services.

I mentioned brevity here to explain it rather than to excuse it. I have rarely had anyone complain that a sermon should have gone on longer, whatever its length.

All of the sermons in this collection were written out in full manuscript form and formatted for oral presentation. As such, you will be reading, presumably in private, what was originally intended to be heard in a very particular public setting: a worship service.

For that reason, you will find sentences that seem to go on forever (and perhaps around in circles a bit)—and words and phrases with punctuation that don't seem to be sentences at all. You will find countless *em-dashes* (long hyphens, as in the one two lines above) scattered about, separating words and phrases. (Actually, you could count them, but I do not think it worth the bother.)

When you find things that don't seem to follow the rules of good grammar, please remember: These sermons were written for people to hear together; not to be read alone.

You will find nouns and pronouns referring to Father, Son and Holy Spirit capitalized throughout—with one exception. It is, of course, no longer the literary convention to capitalize in this way, but I chose to continue the practice I was taught as a child. You may find that this approach to capitalizing has the practical benefit of providing greater clarity when more than one referent is possible. The exception I mentioned above relates to quoting copyrighted translations. When I am quoting, I reproduce the biblical text as originally published.

The footnotes are a later addition to the sermons. I hope you find them helpful and not too distracting. Scripture references include specific versions when I am quoting directly. When I paraphrase or allude to a passage, no version is indicated. I also provide scripture references to indicate the biblical authority for theological assertions I make in the sermons.

I have used a number of translations throughout. In most cases, the sermons were based on whatever version was used as the "pew Bible" in the chapel or church where they were to be preached. One translation I used frequently is no longer available for publication. I have substituted the English Standard Version for it.

I have compiled several indices of the type I would have liked to have found in books of sermons I used in my own preparations and devotions over the years. I hope these lists will prove useful for you as you navigate around the book.

Obviously, this is not a book where you should feel compelled to start at the beginning and read to the end, as you might a novel. Go where you wish, when you wish. And stay as long as you want wherever you are.

I have compiled this and the other books in the series with other preachers in mind. I have been inspired by the ideas and phrasing of many preachers and teachers over the years. I hope something in these pages may inspire, instruct, or at least intrigue someone who is still preparing sermons.

But, of course, sermons aren't written (just) for those who write sermons. I probably gained more from preparing my sermons than anybody else did from hearing them, but some have indicated over the years that they found them helpful. And so I offer them to you now with the prayer that they may bless you, too.

ঙ্ক–৵

# Sermons

# From the Gospel of Luke

## Luke 2:22-40 ESV

Jesus was born as the answer to the prayers of many. He was born into a Jewish family and into the Jewish heritage. Within days of His birth, His family was ensuring that He would be raised according to that heritage in order that He might grow up to fulfill it.

ॐ

*<sup></sup>22 And when the time came for their purification according to the Law of Moses, they brought [Jesus] up to Jerusalem to present him to the Lord 23 (as it is written in the Law of the Lord, "Every male who first opens the womb shall be called holy to the Lord") 24 and to offer a sacrifice according to what is said in the Law of the Lord, "a pair of turtledoves, or two young pigeons." 25 Now there was a man in Jerusalem, whose name was Simeon, and this man was righteous and devout, waiting for the consolation of Israel, and the Holy Spirit was upon him. 26 And it had been revealed to him by the Holy Spirit that he would not see death before he had seen the Lord's Christ. 27 And he came in the Spirit into the temple, and when the parents brought in the child Jesus, to do for him according to the custom of the Law, 28 he took him up in his arms and blessed God and said,*

*29 "Lord, now you are letting your servant depart in peace, according to your word; 30 for my eyes have seen your salvation 31 you have prepared in the presence of all peoples, 32 a light for revelation to the Gentiles, and for glory to your people Israel."*

*33 And his father and his mother marveled at what was said about him. 34 And Simeon blessed them and said to Mary his mother, "Behold, this child is appointed for the fall and rising of many in Israel, and for a sign that is opposed 35 (and a sword will pierce through your own soul also), so that thoughts from many hearts may be revealed."*

*36 And there was a prophetess, Anna, the daughter of Phanuel, of the tribe of Asher. She was advanced in years, having lived with her husband seven years from when she was a virgin, 37 and then as a widow until she was eighty-four. She did not depart from the temple, worshiping with fasting and prayer night*

5

and day. *[38] And coming up at that very hour she began to give thanks to God and to speak of him to all who were waiting for the redemption of Jerusalem.*

*[39] And when they had performed everything according to the Law of the Lord, they returned into Galilee, to their own town of Nazareth. [40] And the child grew and became strong, filled with wisdom. And the favor of God was upon him.*

ର‍ୋ‑ଏ

# 1.

## Small Starts

### Luke 2:22-40 ESV

The salvation of the world started small—given how long God had been getting it ready.[1] Pushing and prodding, pleading with and prophesying to His people across the centuries, God had invested a lot of time and effort to get these people ready for their redemption.[2] They were expecting a big show, whenever it finally came.[3] They had been waiting a long time.[4]

And then one day, the waiting was over. God started saving the world. But He started small. He started as a Baby, born to a young girl of no importance to anybody—anybody human, anyway.[5] He was born in a place not likely to impress anybody—unless you're impressed by stables with straw and stalls and a stray animal here or there.[6] He was born just like everybody else.[7] It was a very small start.

---

[1] Matthew 25:34.
[2] Psalm 34:22.
[3] Isaiah 45:17; Micah 7:7.
[4] Lamentations 3:26.
[5] Luke 1:26-35.
[6] Luke 2:4-7.
[7] Galatians 4:4.

And then a funny thing started to happen. People started to take notice of this small start: shepherds first,[8] then foreign stargazers.[9] The local king and his loyal priests told the foreigners *they* wanted to go and see the salvation Baby.[10] After all, the Baby and His family were only about six miles away.[11] But when this Baby was brought to the city of the king and the Temple of the priests just a few days later, these very big people didn't notice Him. He was just a Baby. He was small.

ॐ•ॐ

But small as He was, He was noticed—this salvation Baby— there in the Jerusalem Temple. A righteous and devout man noticed Him—this Baby Who was bringing salvation to the world. Simeon, righteous and devout and filled with the Holy Spirit (at a time when the Holy Spirit wasn't filling too many people—in Jerusalem or anywhere)—Simeon noticed because he was looking for God's salvation—with the Holy Spirit's help.

Since it was God's salvation coming to earth, God knew what it was going to look like. And God showed Simeon what it looked like. So Simeon recognized God's salvation when he saw it. It looked just like a Baby named Jesus. It was a small start, but seeing it was enough to satisfy Simeon.

Of course, he wasn't just satisfied; he was thrilled—inspired— beside himself with excitement because he knew himself to be beside the Savior of the world. Simeon looked into the face of Jesus and understood that what he was looking at was not just another Jewish baby; he was looking into the face of *"God with us"*[12]—he was looking into the face of God saving him and God

---

8 Luke 2:8-20.

9 Matthew 2:1-2, 11.

10 Matthew 2:3-8.

11 G. W. Van Beek, "Bethlehem," *The Interpreter's Dictionary of the Bible, Vol. 1*, New York, NY: Abingdon Press, p. 394.

12 Matthew 1:23.

saving everyone else who would look into that Face and see what Simeon saw.

That's how it always starts—God's salvation. It starts when a man or woman, boy or girl looks into the face of Jesus and sees the salvation of God.[13]

Of course, not everyone is as righteous as Simeon—as well qualified to see what a small start of this kind really means. In fact, the Bible says there is no one who is righteous—no one[14]—which is the whole point of the salvation we're looking for—that *everybody* is looking for, whether we realize it or not.[15] We're looking for what we don't have—what we don't have and desperately need.

Simeon was looking for God's salvation in God's house— which makes pretty good sense. He was looking for it in God's house because, in addition to being more righteous than most, he was also devout—he was devoted to the God Who had been promising for so long that the salvation of the world was coming. And so when God put His Holy Spirit on Simeon, Simeon got the message and got on up to the Temple to look for God's salvation.

And guess what?

He found it.

❧

God's house is a great place to find God's salvation. Know why? Because people like Simeon—people who are also righteous and devout and filled with the Holy Spirit—people like Mary and Joseph—bring the Jesus Who has been born to them to God's house.

They bring Him other places, too, of course. People like Mary and Joseph bring Jesus into their homes. After they brought Him

---

13 John 6:40.
14 Romans 3:10.
15 John 4:5-15.

to God's house, the Bible says that Mary and Joseph took the Baby born to set God's people free from their sins home.[16]

And though this is how it all starts, with the little baby Jesus being brought to His Father's house to be seen by saints like Simeon, Jesus will go other places as He gets bigger. He will go places that aren't particularly pious.[17] Jesus will go into houses that are not hardly at all like God's house because saving the world is not just about saving the Simeons of the world, those waiting patiently and prayerfully for salvation.

It's also about saving the rigorously un-righteous and the decidedly un-devout and the happily un-holy spirits[18] who are looking for salvation in all the wrong places because they don't realize that what they're after in life is something that only the God Who had Himself born as a Baby can bring.

❧

And finally, the Savior of the world will go where others force Him to go—to courts of justice (or in-justice),[19] to torture chambers[20] and a hill crowded with crosses,[21] and to a cave carved out for corpses.[22] The little Baby born to save the world will grow up to be the God-Man Who does save it—just as Simeon foresaw.

But the birth of a Baby—even a Baby born to a virgin and bearing the very nature of God[23]—is a pitifully small way to start saving the world. For that matter, so is letting brutal men put You to death to the soundtrack of Your enemies' scorn[24] while Your

---

[16] Matthew 2:19-23; Luke 2:39.
[17] Matthew 9:10.
[18] Matthew 9:13; Luke 5:31; 19:10.
[19] John 18:28-38.
[20] Matthew 26:67; 27:30; John 19:1-3.
[21] Matthew 19:16-18.
[22] John 19:38-42.
[23] Hebrews 1:3.
[24] Mark 15:31.

pitifully small band of followers hide in terror while thinking what they're seeing is the end of the world.[25]

Of course, those formerly demoralized and defeated disciples, no larger in number than you in this room, did stand up one day in the streets of Jerusalem and start telling total strangers that a murdered Man is the Savior of the world[26]—that He is God's Savior of the world because, even though He was killed, He isn't actually dead any more,[27] and though He was a Man, He is also God.[28] But even that was a ridiculously small start, really.

❧

This whole salvation business would be pitifully small—if it weren't God Who was doing the saving.

But God *is* the One doing the saving. And the Baby He was born to be grew from that helpless infancy into a unique-in-all-the-world Individual of spiritual strength, divine wisdom and saving grace. His simple words set hearts on fire.[29] His miraculous touch healed bodies and souls.[30] And His mortal death? It was merely prelude to an immortal re-birth in resurrection.[31]

That small start set something monumental in motion. His pathetic pack of followers came alive—with Him and through Him—and reported with the power of the Holy Spirit what they had seen in Jesus—a reborn Jesus. And they told the story so effectively that people all over the world, and all down through history, have seen what they saw, and what Simeon saw in the Temple when Mary and Joseph brought the Baby Jesus in. They—we—have seen the salvation of the Lord.

---

[25] Mark 14:50.
[26] Acts 2:1-4.
[27] Acts 2:22-24.
[28] Colossians 1:15-20.
[29] John 6:67-68; Luke 24:32.
[30] Matthew 4:24.
[31] Acts 2:32; Romans 8:34.

Having the salvation of the world begin with the birth of a Baby seems like an incredibly small start for something so cosmically and eternally important. Having that salvation begin millions of times by someone who has seen Jesus and recognized Him as the Savior telling someone else about it so that that someone else may see it, too, is also a small start for the salvation God brings to His Creation.

But that's how God has chosen to save the world, and because God is doing the saving, even that pitifully small witness that you or I offer is the beginning of that someone else's salvation, which is an essential part of the salvation of the world.

Simeon embraced Jesus and proclaimed Him *"the Salvation of God,"* as small as Jesus was. Small starts—but don't be fooled: God was—is—saving the world. Your relationship with Jesus may start small. But it won't stay that way, not if you see Him for Who He is: your Salvation.

ক্ত

## Luke 2:41-52 ESV

*[41] Now [Jesus'] parents went to Jerusalem every year at the Feast of the Passover. [42] And when he was twelve years old, they went up according to custom. [43] And when the feast was ended, as they were returning, the boy Jesus stayed behind in Jerusalem. His parents did not know it, [44] but supposing him to be in the group they went a day's journey, but then they began to search for him among their relatives and acquaintances, [45] and when they did not find him, they returned to Jerusalem, searching for him. [46] After three days they found him in the temple, sitting among the teachers, listening to them and asking them questions. [47] And all who heard him were amazed at his understanding and his answers. [48] And when his parents saw him, they were astonished. And his mother said to him, "Son, why have you treated us so? Behold, your father and I have been searching for you in great distress." [49] And he said to them, "Why were you looking for me? Did you not know that I must be in my Father's house?" [50] And they did not understand the saying that he spoke to them. [51] And he went down with them and came to Nazareth and was submissive to them. And his mother treasured up all these things in her heart.*

*[52] And Jesus increased in wisdom and in stature and in favor with God and man.*

ॐ≺

# 2.

# Looking for Jesus—Finding the Christ

## Luke 2:41-52 ESV

Have you ever noticed how time hurries by during the holidays? For instance, on Friday, Jesus was a newborn Baby. Today,[32] He's a twelve-year-old Boy.

His parents must have thought, as many of us do watching kids grow up, "Where did the time go?" After their journey to Jerusalem for the Passover holiday, Mary and Joseph were also wondering, "Where did *He* go?"

It just goes to show that even the best parents—the best parents of all time—can have some bad moments. The man and woman closer to Jesus than anyone else in all the world—the people who know Him better than anybody—all of a sudden realize they've lost sight of Him.

Rarely has He been out of their sight since the holy night He was born to them. But if He isn't right there with them now, they're confident He's nearby, in the midst of their broader family or community who care for Him just as much as they do.

---

[32] This sermon was preached on Sunday, December 27th.

You go with Jesus to and through a wonderful religious ritual. You're on your way back home—back to the normal routine. You're still feeling the joy of what you've just experienced.

How could Jesus not be with you?

And yet, there you are one day—the muster sheets are complete, and Jesus simply isn't anywhere you expect Him to be. That Mary and Joseph can't find Him *one time* is surprising enough that it's worth mentioning in the Bible. But if you and I are honest, we lose track of Jesus a lot more often than that.

After a big holiday—or any old day—you can get so distracted or disgruntled or depressed that your point of view just doesn't have room for Jesus. All you can see is yourself and your concerns—or other people and theirs—looming larger than life—and certainly larger than they or you ever deserve to be—or should be allowed to be—if you're not to lose sight of Jesus.

Or maybe there's no negligence involved at all. Maybe for no reason you can discern, Jesus just isn't "there."

He said that He would be *"with you always."*[33]

So where is He?

Mary and Joseph know Jesus isn't where they thought He would be—where they want Him to be—which is with them—so they do the most logical thing: They go looking for Him. And in doing so, they have set all of us who lose track of Jesus a good example: If you can't find Jesus, go looking for Him. Don't just assume He'll turn up, sooner or later. That's too big a risk.

Mary and Joseph stop what they're doing. They turn around from where they've been going. They leave the people they've been hanging out with. And they go looking for Jesus.

Now let's be honest, the method Mary and Joseph use is more like looking for a needle in a haystack. They clearly don't know how to conduct a systematic search in an efficient and effective manner. They canvas the vast capital city of Jerusalem for days,

---

[33] Matthew 28:20, ESV.

hoping to happen upon one particular 12-year-old Boy. They don't have a clue what they're doing. But, in time, God guides them to Jesus anyway.

It's amazing how long it takes Mary and Joseph to think to look for Jesus in the Temple—the house of God. Where else are they looking—and why? They've been told by angels Who He is. They know what He's here for. "Why didn't you know where to find Me?" says Jesus. *"I must be in my Father's house. I must be about my Father's business."*

৵৽

We'll get back to that—but notice that what they learn when they do find Jesus can teach you a lot about how to go looking for Jesus more effectively when you realize that's what you need to be doing. If you're looking for Jesus, the house of God is a pretty good place to *start* your search. *"I must be in my Father's house."*

The Temple in Jerusalem is long gone, of course. It was already gone—destroyed—even before Luke wrote his Gospel.

This church will do well enough now. It, too, is the Father's house, though on a significantly simpler scale. Our Heavenly Father has chosen to make His presence felt here—to cause His Holy Spirit to hover about us and His holy Word to be hidden within us. This is a good place—though not at all the only place—to look for Jesus successfully.

The key, of course, is to actually look. There were apparently quite a few people who went to the Jerusalem Temple who weren't really looking for Jesus—when He was a Baby—or a Boy—or a Man in His full maturity.

Old Simeon and Anna were looking for Him, of course[34]—as were Mary and Joseph, as we've read. Pilgrims were enthusiastically looking for Him when He showed up there for His last

---

[34] Luke 2:22-40.

Passover[35]—though the money-changers and the chief priests, just as surely, were not.[36]

Many people today—it seems—have no interest in looking for Jesus, and that's a shame—and worse. Everybody who realizes that Jesus is not "there" should be looking for Jesus. You can't make them look if they don't want to, of course, but you could encourage them to want to—at least a little.

And let me let you in on a little secret: A lot of people may tell you they're not looking for Jesus, but an awful lot of people are looking for *something* today—desperately looking. And though the one thing they're sure of is that Jesus is not What or Who they're looking for—they're actually wrong. Most people who are looking for things like "Mr. Right," or "love in all the wrong places," or "answers," won't find what they're looking for without finding Jesus first.

Neither you nor anyone else will be "right" until you find Jesus and let Him make you "right." Every place you look for love will be the wrong place unless you find Jesus there, too.

And the only answers worth finding in this life are the ones you find when you find Him.

And why is that?

Because when you go looking for Jesus, Who you find is Christ.

Mary and Joseph go back to Jerusalem to look for their 12-year-old Son. Three days later, they discover a Boy in the Temple Who bears a striking resemblance to *their* Boy, yet the Boy they find in the Temple is astonishing the greatest theologians of the day—and them. The tenured teachers are teaching, but this Boy's questions indicate that He is way ahead of them.

They are scholars, well-versed in the Law; He is the Savior, a Son sent from the God Who gave them the Law.

---

[35] Matthew 21:9.
[36] Luke 19:45-48.

Mary points to Joseph beside her and tells Jesus, "Your father and I were distressed when You weren't where we thought You would be." And Jesus points heavenward and replies, "My Father knows where I am and that I am exactly where He wants Me to be."

They've been looking for their Son, Jesus. They find *God's* Son—the Christ.

ॐ∽

What are you looking for when you come to this place? What are you looking for when you lift your heart in worship or bow your head in prayer? What are you looking for when you read what Jesus said and did in the Bible, or copy Him, as best you can, in your own words and deeds?

By all means, look for Jesus when you feel like you've lost Him. And don't be surprised if Jesus doesn't "stay where you put Him." Just realize that when you look for Jesus, God intends that you will find His Christ—not just a nice Boy—or Man—Who will keep you company and calms your fears as you travel through "this world of woe."[37]

You will find the Christ Who has amazing answers that will overwhelm your most curious questions. You will find the Christ Who will take your mind and heart and soul far beyond man's understanding of religious things to revelations of holy things only heaven can conceive. God will give you a Christ Who, though first a Baby, and then a Boy—became a Man Whose sacrificial death destroyed the hold of sin over your life and every life, now and forever.

Mary says to Jesus, *"Son, why have you treated us so?"*

Jesus answers her, *"Why were you looking for me."*

It's an odd exchange for a 12-year-old boy to have with his mother, under the (human) circumstances. It just goes to show that

---

[37] From the traditional folk/gospel song, "Wayfarin' Stranger," circa early 1800s.

even those who think they know Jesus best still have a lot to learn about Him.

And for His part, Jesus doesn't understand why they, of all people, didn't come to God's house first to find Him. The best and most effective way to look for Jesus is to understand that Who He is will determine where He will be.

ॐ◌ॐ

But there's more to it than that.

You see, you may think that you are the one looking for Jesus when you sense the emptiness only He can fill. But the truth is that long before you ever thought of looking for Jesus—and many times when you don't think of looking for Him now—Jesus is looking for you. That's what God sent Him to do— *"to seek and to save that which was lost"*[38]—as the King James puts it.

Jesus doesn't get lost. He is always where God wants Him to be—always being the Christ God sent Him into this life to be.[39] And the Christ Who is Jesus is always looking for you—to accomplish your salvation—your redemption and transformation and reconciliation with God. And in the course of this lifelong searching of Jesus Christ for you, He will cause you to feel the joy and wonder of being found by the God Who refuses to give up in His search for you, wherever you go—whatever you've done.[40]

Mary and Joseph go looking for their Jesus and they find so very much more—so much more that they will have to think for quite a while about the meaning of those three days when they thought they had lost Him—which is okay, because they are going to have an eternity to do so, because they have let their Christ find them.

---

[38] Luke 19:10, KJV.
[39] 1 John 4:14.
[40] Matthew 18:12.

The Boy Jesus goes home with His human parents, which suggests a happy ending to this biblical story: They have found each other.

And years later, when the disciples of a very grown-up Jesus—including Mary, His mother—come to the end of another Passover in Jerusalem and think—for an agonizing three days—that they have lost Jesus for good, perhaps the memory of His boyhood assurance to her that He has to be about His Father's business encourages her to keep looking for her Jesus, until she finds her (resurrected) Christ—or He finds her—again and forever.

పోం

## Luke 3:15-17, 21-22 NRSV

[15] *As the people were filled with expectation, and all were questioning in their hearts concerning John, whether he might be the Messiah,* [16] *John answered all of them by saying, "I baptize you with water; but one who is more powerful than I is coming; I am not worthy to untie the thong of his sandals. He will baptize you with the Holy Spirit and fire.* [17] *His winnowing fork is in his hand, to clear his threshing floor and to gather the wheat into his granary; but the chaff he will burn with unquenchable fire."*

[21] *Now when all the people were baptized, and when Jesus also had been baptized and was praying, the heaven was opened,* [22] *and the Holy Spirit descended upon him in bodily form like a dove. And a voice came from heaven, "You are my Son, the Beloved; with you I am well pleased."*

❧

# 3.

# Just Getting Started

## Luke 3:15-17, 21-22 NRSV

Mary Poppins used to say, "Well begun is half done."[41]

To do anything, you have to *start* doing it. This sounds rather obvious, but the importance of starting cannot be overemphasized. How many great things—and how many more simply good things—never happened because some group, or even some individual, just never started to do them?

The baptism of Jesus is the start of His ministry. It doesn't seem like much, compared to what comes after. Jesus merely goes down to the Jordan River where John is baptizing and gets in line.

But don't sell that short. To be there, Jesus has to leave behind the familiar, the comfortable, the predictable and controllable life He has been living. He has "arisen"—as the Bible likes to say— and set off down a different road. He has taken the first step without which all that will follow could not happen. It is a start.

And God affirms His start. Jesus has not yet done anything earth-shaking. No lepers have been healed[42]—no multitudes fed.[43]

---

[41] I always associated the "proverb" with the 1964 Walt Disney movie, *Mary Poppins*. I have subsequently learned that Aristotle quoted it prior to 322 B.C.
[42] Mark 1:40-42.
[43] Matthew 14:16-21.

Jesus has not yet picked a disciple[44] or told a parable[45] or calmed a storm.[46] And yet, as He comes up out of the waters of baptism, Jesus experiences a dramatic, divine confirmation of Who He is and what He has done. God approves of what Jesus has started.

Starting His ministry—starting what God sent Him to do—is enough for God to speak to Jesus and claim Jesus as His Son, just as God claimed Him through the angel who announced the miraculous conception of Jesus to Mary.[47] Starting His ministry is enough for God to send the Holy Spirit to Jesus to enable Him to do all that He will do—now that He has started.

We, of course, know what's going to happen. We know because it has happened. We know, now that Jesus has started His ministry in the waters of the Jordan, that He will, one day, be able to say, *"It is finished!"*[48] having won our salvation on the Cross.[49]

But for Jesus, none of this has happened. Nothing is guaranteed. It all depends on His starting—His taking the first step.

And He does start. And though He has not picked a disciple, He soon will. Jesus will pick 12 disciples and then more. And each disciple will then have to start—each will have to take a first step of faith in order to follow Jesus. And when a disciple steps out in faith, God will confirm that simple action—God will pour out His Holy Spirit to empower the next step—and the next—along this new road of faith and fellowship and service—this following in the footsteps of Jesus.[50]

What is it in your spiritual journey—the ministry God has created you to accomplish—that you need to start? What awaits your first step?

---

44 Matthew 3:18-22.
45 Mark 4:2.
46 Mark 4:35-39.
47 Luke 1:26-35.
48 John 19:30.
49 Colossians 1:20.
50 1 Peter 2:21.

This will be a great year—for God's work—for our Chapel—for you—if you start. You will read the Bible through this year—if you start. You will deepen your prayer life—if you start.

You will mend broken relationships—if you start. You will walk closer to Christ—if you start.

"Oh, if only the heavens would open and God would speak a word of affirmation and affection to me and send His Holy Spirit to strengthen and reassure me! Then I could start."

Sorry, that's not how it works. God calls, and when you step out in faith—when you start just because God has told you to—then, like Jesus, you will hear and see and know God's confirmation.

In Christ, well begun is better than half done. In Christ, well begun is affirmed with God's *"Well done!"* Step out in faith and you will hear God's joyful, "You are My beloved child; with you I am well pleased."

Let's get started.

శ్రాం

## Luke 4:1-13 NRSV

¹ *Jesus, full of the Holy Spirit, returned from the Jordan and was led by the Spirit in the wilderness,* ² *where for forty days he was tempted by the devil. He ate nothing at all during those days, and when they were over, he was famished.* ³ *The devil said to him, "If you are the Son of God, command this stone to become a loaf of bread."*

⁴ *Jesus answered him, "It is written,*

> *'One does not live by bread alone.'"*

⁵ *Then the devil led him up and showed him in an instant all the kingdoms of the world.* ⁶ *And the devil said to him, "To you I will give their glory and all this authority; for it has been given over to me, and I give it to anyone I please.* ⁷ *If you, then, will worship me, it will all be yours."*

⁸ *Jesus answered him, "It is written,*

> *'Worship the Lord your God,*
> *and serve only him.'"*

⁹ *Then the devil took him to Jerusalem, and placed him on the pinnacle of the temple, saying to him, "If you are the Son of God, throw yourself down from here,* ¹⁰ *for it is written,*

> *'He will command his angels concerning you,*
> *to protect you,'*

¹¹ *and*

> *'On their hands they will bear you up,*
> *so that you will not dash your foot against a stone.'"*

¹² *Jesus answered him, "It is said,*

> *'Do not put the Lord your God to the test.'"*

¹³ *When the devil had finished every test, he departed from him until an opportune time.*

❧

# 4.

# Until an Opportune Time

## Luke 4:1-13 NRSV

You may have a hard time getting your mind around great theological concepts like election and justification, pre-destination and sanctification, but when the Bible talks about "temptation," the fog clears. You know exactly what it means: *"[E]very man is tempted,"*[51] says James.

Jesus was tempted. The Bible says, *"[He] was in all points tempted like as we are, yet without sin."*[52] We just heard that Jesus *"was led into the wilderness where for forty days he was tempted by the devil."* It's a dramatic encounter, and we can go a long way toward defeating the devil in our lives by doing what Jesus did.

But notice that when Jesus outdid the devil in the desert, the tempting wasn't over. Even as the Bible is celebrating our Lord's victory—*"When the devil finished every test, he departed from him..."*— the story concludes on an ominous note: *"...until an opportune time."*

৵৵৶

---

[51] James 1:14, KJV.
[52] Hebrews 4:15, KJV.

What is "an opportune time" for temptation? The word "opportune" means "suitable" or "convenient." It's when the opportunity exists. Even Jesus could not eliminate "opportune times" for temptation in His life, though He certainly minimized them.

Jesus would face other temptations throughout His ministry, and they would come in different forms. Opponents would confront Him and try to trip Him up.[53] Modern translations say they "tested" Him, but the King James says they "tempted" Him, and there is insight in that translation. There is a subtle but dangerous temptation in conflict, even when you are able to avoid the trap being set for you.

Conflict is an opportune time for temptation.

∂∽∾

So is success.

When Jesus healed the sick and fed the hungry crowds, they wanted to put Him on a throne—their throne.[54] When the Palm Sunday pilgrims proclaim Jesus king, His climbing up on the back of a donkey[55] is His way of resisting the temptation of misappropriating His success in the service of God.

∂∽∾

And then there is danger.

As Jesus approached the hour of His arrest in the Garden of Gethsemane,[56] the devil found the most opportune time of all for temptation. "Save your life" is a pretty compelling temptation. In fact, it is only a temptation when there is a more compelling reason to give your life.

---

[53] Matthew 16:1; 19:3; 22:35.
[54] John 6:15.
[55] Matthew 21:7.
[56] Matthew 26:36-46.

And in this case, there was. When Jesus prayed, *"Not My will, but Thine, be done,"*[57] He was accepting God's mission for Him and, at the same time, pulling the plug on temptation's opportune time.

ॐ

So what about your battles with temptation?

First of all, don't surrender before the battle starts. Paul says, *"God is faithful; he will not let you be tempted beyond what you can bear. …he will …provide a way out"*[58] Every temptation can be resisted.

James says, *"…count it all joy when ye fall into…temptations."*[59] Not because you will enjoy being tempted, but because the experience of temptation shows that the devil sees you as a worthwhile target for his attention. And you can rejoice when you experience temptation because when you endure it—resist it—God will reward you. James says you will *"…receive the crown of life, which the Lord has promised to those who love him."*[60]

And here's some even better news: *"The Lord know[s] how to deliver the godly out of temptations,"*[61] according to Peter. *"Because [Jesus] himself suffered when he was tempted, he is able to help those who are being tempted."*[62] Jesus told the disciples, *"Watch and pray, that you do not enter into temptation…."*[63] And He taught them to pray: *"…lead us not into temptation, but deliver us from evil."*[64]

ॐ

The "watch" part is there, too. Pay attention to your life so that you recognize your "opportune times" for temptation to bubble up. Be on guard when you encounter conflict, find your ego

---

[57] Matthew 26:39, KJV.
[58] 1 Corinthians 10:13, NIV.
[59] James 1:2, KJV.
[60] James 1:12, ESV.
[61] 2 Peter 2:9, KJV.
[62] Hebrews 2:18, NIV.
[63] Matthew 26:41, RSV.
[64] Matthew 6:13, ESV.

expanding, or feel afraid. Make sure you desire the things of God more than your own selfish desires.

Look at the temptation from God's perspective, and at yourself as someone the devil wants to tempt because he identifies you with Jesus. Visualize the holy joy that will be yours when you successfully resist the evil one, which you can do. *"Resist the devil,"* says James, *"and he will flee from you."*[65]

Temptation is not sin, and it need not cause you to sin. Be strong in the Lord, watch and pray—and let God do the rest.

ও০৫

---

[65] James 4:7, ESV.

## Hebrews 4:14-16 ESV

The Book of Hebrews is a systematic argument for the superiority of Christianity. A part of that argument is that Jesus Christ, the Christian's High Priest, is infinitely superior to human priests serving in earthly temples. And one of the reasons that Jesus is superior to all other priests is that, though tempted like us, He never sinned.

৯৽৽৻

*[14] Since then we have a great high priest who has passed through the heavens, Jesus, the Son of God, let us hold fast our confession. [15] For we do not have a high priest who is unable to sympathize with our weaknesses, but one who in every respect has been tempted as we are, yet without sin. [16] Let us then with confidence draw near to the throne of grace, that we may receive mercy and find grace to help in time of need.*

৯৽৽৻

## Luke 4:1-13 ESV

The first three Gospels provide a detailed example of the kind of temptation Jesus underwent—and overcame. These temptations took place early in the ministry of Jesus.

൭᠊ᡐ

*¹ And Jesus, full of the Holy Spirit, returned from the Jordan and was led by the Spirit in the wilderness ² for forty days, being tempted by the devil. And he ate nothing during those days. And when they were ended, he was hungry. ³ The devil said to him, "If you are the Son of God, command this stone to become bread."*

*⁴ And Jesus answered him, "It is written,*

*'Man shall not live by bread alone.'"*

*⁵ And the devil took him up and showed him all the kingdoms of the world in a moment of time, ⁶ and said to him, "To you I will give all this authority and their glory, for it has been delivered to me, and I give it to whom I will. ⁷ If you, then, will worship me, it will all be yours."*

*⁸ And Jesus answered him, "It is written,*

*"'You shall worship the Lord your God,*

*and him only shall you serve.'"*

*⁹ And he took him to Jerusalem and set him on the pinnacle of the temple and said to him, "If you are the Son of God, throw yourself down from here, ¹⁰ for it is written,*

*"'He will command his angels concerning you,*

*to guard you,'*

*¹¹ and*

*"'On their hands they will bear you up,*

*lest you strike your foot against a stone.'"*

*¹² And Jesus answered him, "It is said,*

*'You shall not put the Lord your God to the test.'"*

*¹³ And when the devil had ended every temptation, he departed from him until an opportune time.*

൭᠊ᡐ

# 5.

# The Road Not (to be) Taken

## Hebrews 4:14-16; Luke 4:1-13 ESV

Here at our church, we encourage the study of the scriptures. We believe it is essential for God's people to read the Bible deeply and systematically, to increase our awareness of its content—and perhaps more importantly, to discover, with ever increasing understanding, the divine messages God is revealing to us in its words.

One of the best ways to uncover the meaning of the Bible is to compare those passages where the same story is told by different authors, and to note the different perspectives—the variations in emphasis. Another way is to compare how different modern versions translate the original language (the Hebrew or Greek) into English. Translation from one language to another always requires some amount of interpretation, because the meanings of words in different languages are seldom (if ever) exactly the same.

One example of a place where both of these Bible study methods come into play is the story of the Temptation of Jesus, told in the first three Gospels. Mark provides only a summary of the Temptation, while Matthew and Luke give very similar accounts of the specific confrontations between Jesus and the devil—similar, but not exact.

At the same time, various translations of Luke's account demonstrate slightly different understandings of what Luke is saying about this important episode in the life of our Savior.

Matthew and Mark seem to see the Holy Spirit pushing or pulling Jesus out of the baptismal waters of the Jordan and into the mountainous Judean desert so that Jesus would be tempted by the devil. The phrase Matthew uses to describe the purpose of the Holy Spirit's leading is *"to be tempted by the devil."*

Even the translation of Luke's account you heard earlier seems to emphasize the same perspective. It says that "Jesus...was led by the Spirit in the desert, *where for forty days he was tempted by the devil"*— as though that was all that was going on out there for almost six weeks.

ক্ক-ড়

But the literal translation of the Greek words in Luke goes like this, *"Jesus, full of the Holy Spirit...was led by the Spirit in the desert forty days, being tempted by the devil."*

Did you catch the difference in emphasis?

For Luke, Jesus went to the desert—spent 40 days in the desert—not for the purpose of debating the devil, but to be led by the Holy Spirit Who had filled Him. Luke says the Spirit led Jesus "in" the desert, not "into" the desert. Luke says the Spirit led Jesus for 40 days.

Yes, the devil tagged along, trying to disrupt the holy process. But it is not until the end of His 40-day retreat with the Spirit that Jesus turns His attention to confronting the devil's temptations.

We'll look at the specific temptations in a moment, but let's look first at the business of temptation in general, using Jesus as our example. Even when Jesus was filled with the Holy Spirit and was being led by the Holy Spirit, He was still being tempted by the devil. And don't suppose this was the first time the devil had tried to "worm" his way into the inner workings of the heart and mind of Jesus.

The passage we heard from Hebrews said that Jesus was *"tempted in every way, just as we are."* Now, my temptations didn't begin when I was 30 years old. They didn't wait till after I was baptized. I can't remember when the devil started tempting me. How about you? And *that's* how early the devil started in on Jesus.

The Gospels say Jesus dealt with the devil's specific temptations in the desert so effectively that the tempter had to take off—for a time. Perhaps James was thinking about this when he wrote, *"Resist the devil, and he will flee from you."*[66]

We'll talk about how to resist effectively in a moment, but let's also be honest with ourselves: The devil may flee for a while, but he always comes back—he certainly did with Jesus. Face it: Temptation is a part of life. It was for Jesus; it is for us.

But listen to what Hebrews says about Jesus and temptation: He *"has been tempted in every way, just as we are—yet was without sin."*

Jesus did not sin—ever! He felt every temptation that everybody else has felt. He faced every temptation known to man—and He did not sin. He never yielded to a single temptation—which is a good thing, because if He had, He wouldn't have done any of us any good.[67] He couldn't have been the acceptable sacrifice for our sins—our failures to resist the temptations the devil dropped on us. So raise a holy cheer for Jesus' perfect record against temptation!

స్త్రీ

Our records, of course, are not perfect. Far from it. We have yielded to the devil's temptations over and over again. We are sinners, saved by the grace of Jesus[68] Who never sinned—but Who *was* tempted.

Let's go back.

---

[66] James 4:7, ESV.

[67] Hebrews 10:11-14.

[68] Ephesians 2:8.

Jesus was tempted, but He did not sin. Therefore, temptation is not the same thing as sin. Being tempted is no more sinful for you than it was for Jesus. Until you yield, you have not sinned. If you do not yield, you do not sin.

But, of course, you have yielded—you have sinned. So have I. But here's another thing about temptation: Sometimes you *don't* yield to it. If you always yielded to temptation—if you *always* sinned and never resisted successfully—then resisting would not be a real option. And there would be no such thing, really, as temptation— the urge to do wrong when you could also do right. If the devil always won....

But he doesn't. We can, and do, resist temptation—not often, perhaps—not often enough, certainly. But if we have resisted temptation—even once—it means we *can* resist temptation. It means we can resist *any* temptation—at least theoretically.

જ≈∽⊛

So how do we improve our records regarding temptation— assuming we want to—which we should, because yielding to temptation—any temptation—yields all kinds of uncomfortable consequences, because, as the old hymn says, "yielding is sin,"[69] and *"the wages of sin* (not to put too fine a point on it) *is death"*?[70]

How do we overcome temptation?

We could "try harder." But that's been tried already—and doesn't work, most of the time.

There's also "calling it something else." But that doesn't work, either. Sin is sin, whatever you call it, and if you yield to it, you get what you got coming. Call it something else and it gets harder to resist temptation, not easier.

So how did Jesus do it? How did Jesus resist temptation?

જ≈∽⊛

---

[69] Horatio R. Palmer, "Yield Not to Temptation," 1868.
[70] Romans 6:23, ESV.

Well, first of all, He was the Son of God, which we aren't. But He was also truly human—and truly tempted—which means He *could* have sinned. But Jesus resisted temptation—period. And Luke provides some of His secrets.

Luke says Jesus was filled with the Holy Spirit. Jesus filled His heart and mind with a Presence infinitely more powerful than the devil.[71] Where the Holy Spirit was, the devil could not go.

Jesus was led by the Holy Spirit that filled Him. Because the Holy Spirit directed the attitudes and actions of Jesus, the deceptive alternatives of the devil never got a chance to be considered as options.

∂•∽

And to come full circle, Jesus was inspired and informed by the Word of God. Jesus read His Bible the same way we are teaching our children and encouraging our adults to do. When the devil tried to tempt Him with, "You ought to do this…," Jesus responded with, "Let's see what God says about that."

And when the devil starts quoting God's Word back to Jesus, Jesus knows enough of its content, and understands its message well enough, that the devil's *misuse* of it doesn't mislead Him.

Now Jesus doesn't say, "I'm smarter than you, devil." Jesus doesn't delude Himself into thinking that He *can't* be tempted—or sin. He just lets God deal with the devil for Him.

As the story is told, it was at the end of the 40 days in the desert that Jesus first responded to a temptation. Maybe it took 40 days with the Holy Spirit before Jesus was sufficiently strengthened and instructed to confront the devil directly, even though the devil had been pestering Him the whole time.

Jesus was hungry, and the devil tried to exploit that hunger: "Do for yourself. Take care of 'Number One.'"

---

[71] 1 John 4:4.

But Jesus understood that God had not sent Him to this world to be "Number One." *"The last shall be first and the first last,"*[72] He said. Jesus also knew that He was not here to do anything for Himself. *"The Son of Man did not come to be served"* (or even to serve Himself), but to serve others *"and to give His life as a ransom for many,"* Jesus told His disciples.[73] Knowing what He knew about what God was doing with Him, Jesus was not tempted by the devil's first temptation.

❦

Nor was He deceived by the second—another common temptation. "I can give you everything You ever wanted."

Of course, the devil doesn't have what Jesus wants. The devil doesn't have what any of us really want. With the devil, it's always "bait and switch" because *"[e]very good...and...perfect gift comes from above,"*[74] which means that every "gift" the devil offers is anything but. But you have to know God's Word to know that.

The third temptation is a bit bizarre: "Jump off the Temple tower and impress the pilgrims with how quickly the angels will arrange Your rescue." And Jesus responds by quoting God's Word to the effect that God is not to be tempted.

What is Jesus saying?

When you tempt God's child, you're messing with God Himself. True of Jesus—true of you and me. When you are tempted, the devil wants you to think that it is just helpless little you left to face the overwhelming evil and inescapable allure of the all-powerful prince of darkness—alone.

❦

But that's a deception, too.

---

[72] Matthew 20:16, ESV.

[73] Matthew 20:28, ESV.

[74] James 1:17, KJV.

Every temptation is a challenge to God Himself, because it is His Spirit that is in you to strengthen you,[75] and His Spirit that is there to lead you out of every temptation,[76] and His Word that is available to you to detect the deceit and defeat the devil—every time. Not you—God. For *"greater is he that is in you, than he that is in the world."*[77]

Jesus rejected the devil's temptations, and His Spirit and His Word will enable you to resist the temptations the devil will try on you.

ॐ∙ॐ

---

75 1 Corinthians 3:16.
76 1 Corinthians 10:13.
77 1 John 4:4, KJV.

## Luke 4:14-21 NRSV

[14] Then Jesus, filled with the power of the Spirit, returned to Galilee, and a report about him spread through all the surrounding country. [15] He began to teach in their synagogues and was praised by everyone.

[16] When he came to Nazareth, where he had been brought up, he went to the synagogue on the sabbath day, as was his custom. He stood up to read, [17] and the scroll of the prophet Isaiah was given to him. He unrolled the scroll and found the place where it was written:

> [18] "The Spirit of the Lord is upon me,
> because he has anointed me
> > to bring good news to the poor.
> He has sent me
> to proclaim release to the captives
> > and recovery of sight to the blind,
> to let the oppressed go free,
> [19] to proclaim the year of the Lord's favor."

[20] And he rolled up the scroll, gave it back to the attendant, and sat down. The eyes of all in the synagogue were fixed on him. [21] Then he began to say to them, "Today this scripture has been fulfilled in your hearing."

❧❦

# 6.

# The Familiar Face You Do Not Know

## Luke 4:14-21 NRSV

You'll be interested to know that Jesus has been spotted. He had disappeared for a while after being baptized in the Jordan River[78]—wandered off into the wilderness somewhere with no word from Him for weeks.[79]

Now, He's turned up again in Galilee. A guy like Jesus can't wander around the towns and villages of Galilee without making an impression.[80] And sooner or later, He was bound to head for His old hometown, Nazareth.

One day in the far distant future, Nazareth will become the capital and largest city in northern Israel. But Nazareth in the time of Jesus is a small town, and, as with all small towns—except, perhaps, our own[81]—everyone knows each other because everyone grew up together.

---

[78] Matthew 3:13-17.
[79] Luke 4:1-13.
[80] Matthew 4:23-25.
[81] This sermon was preached in a church in Pinehurst, North Carolina, a small town to which many people from other parts of the country retire.

Jesus walks into Nazareth and knows every rock in the road and every urchin at His heels. He knows every house in the village about as well as He knows the one He grew up in.

On the Sabbath, Jesus walks into the synagogue just as He has done all His life and He knows every face looking back at Him from the hard, stone seats around the walls. The old men have watched Jesus grow up and taught Him in this very synagogue. The young men have been his friends and childhood playmates.

The boys, wide-eyed and fidgeting, have run errands for Jesus and watched Him work. He knows these people—and they know Him.

Jesus is a 30-year-old man. He has sat in this synagogue hundreds of times, listening as the men of Nazareth say their prayers and sing the psalms—as they read the scripture and give their interpretation of what they have read. Jesus Himself has prayed and sung, read and reflected upon the text when it was His turn to do so. They know the sound of His voice and how well He can sing. They know what He's had to say about any number of passages in their Bible. The men of Nazareth know this Jesus of Nazareth—or think they do.

They gather in their familiar place of worship and look at the familiar face of Jesus and wait for a word they expect to be familiar, too.

But today will be different. Jesus reads a familiar passage and proceeds to tell them that they didn't really know Him at all.

༄

Today, the Spirit of the Lord is upon Him. Today, He is filled with the power of God. Today, in their synagogue, Jesus of Nazareth, Jesus of their village, Jesus of their simple and settled understanding, announces that He is God's anointed—God's Messiah. Jesus, the old friend, the comfortable companion, the familiar face, is actually the Bringer of the greatest good news in the world, the Releaser of captives, the Healer of the blind and the Free-er of the oppressed.

You can be sure that *that* revelation caused a few of them to lose their place in the liturgy: "What is good old Jesus doing? What's got into Him?"

Can you hear their minds at work?

"Settle down, Jesus. We know Who You are and what You're supposed to say and how You're supposed to act."

Instead, Jesus stands up in the midst of the people who know Him best and issues His own personal and spiritual declaration of independence: "I am and will be what God has called Me and caused Me to be. Today, I announce to you, in this place where you have come to think you know all about Me, that you don't know Me at all—unless you know Me in the power that God has given Me—as the One God has sent to do the things He wants His Messiah to do."

❧

That's what happened in the synagogue in Nazareth. Here we are in this church in Pinehurst, as is our custom on a Sunday morning. For us, Jesus is as familiar as the service we share. He's always here, sharing our prayers and songs, our word and sacrament. Familiar, predictable, comfortable.

But today could be the day when He opens the scripture and speaks a word of incredible power and revelation to you, confronting you with a Jesus you only thought you knew.

The prophet Isaiah foresaw a Messiah, filled with the Spirit, fulfilling God's promise to those who most need His grace. And old familiar Jesus stood up one day in Nazareth and shocked His friends by saying, *"Today this promise is fulfilled in your hearing."*

What is He saying to you today?

❧

**Isaiah 53:1-3 ESV**

Isaiah prophesied about a special servant of God Who would serve God faithfully, even though he would suffer greatly in doing so. In fact, the suffering was the service that would make the servant special to God, even though people who saw him suffer though it was a sign that God had rejected him—and they treated the servant of God accordingly.

ॐ—ॐ

> ¹ *Who has believed what he has heard from us?*
>   *And to whom has the arm of the* LORD *been revealed?*
> ² *For he grew up before him like a young plant,*
>   *and like a root out of dry ground;*
> *he had no form or majesty that we should look at him,*
>   *and no beauty that we should desire him.*
> ³ *He was despised and rejected by men,*
>   *a man of sorrows and acquainted with grief;*
> *and as one from whom men hide their faces*
>   *he was despised, and we esteemed him not.*

ॐ—ॐ

## Luke 4:16-30 ESV

Jesus grew up in the village of Nazareth, but moved to Capernaum when He began His ministry. In the early days, Jesus visited and spoke in the synagogues around Galilee. One day, He returned to His hometown and spoke to a roomful of familiar faces. Their response was a preview of His whole ministry.

৵৹৻

*$^{16}$ And [Jesus] came to Nazareth, where he had been brought up. And as was his custom, he went to the synagogue on the Sabbath day, and he stood up to read. $^{17}$ And the scroll of the prophet Isaiah was given to him. He unrolled the scroll and found the place where it was written,*
*$^{18}$ "The Spirit of the Lord is upon me,*
*because he has anointed me*
*to proclaim good news to the poor.*
*He has sent me*
*to proclaim liberty to the captives*
*and recovering of sight to the blind,*
*to set at liberty those who are oppressed,*
*$^{19}$ to proclaim the year of the Lord's favor."*
*$^{20}$ And he rolled up the scroll and gave it back to the attendant and sat down. And the eyes of all in the synagogue were fixed on him. $^{21}$ And he began to say to them, "Today this Scripture has been fulfilled in your hearing." $^{22}$ And all spoke well of him and marveled at the gracious words that were coming from his mouth. And they said, "Is not this Joseph's son?" $^{23}$ And he said to them, "Doubtless you will quote to me this proverb, '"Physician, heal yourself." What we have heard you did at Capernaum, do here in your hometown as well.'" $^{24}$ And he said, "Truly, I say to you, no prophet is acceptable in his hometown. $^{25}$ But in truth, I tell you, there were many widows in Israel in the days of Elijah, when the heavens were shut up three years and six months, and a great famine came over all the land, $^{26}$ and Elijah was sent to none of them but only to Zarephath, in the land of Sidon, to a woman who was a widow. $^{27}$ And there were many lepers in Israel in the time of the prophet Elisha, and none of them was cleansed, but only Naaman the Syrian."*

*[28] When they heard these things, all in the synagogue were filled with wrath. [29] And they rose up and drove him out of the town and brought him to the brow of the hill on which their town was built, so that they could throw him down the cliff. [30] But passing through their midst, he went away.*

❧

# 7.

# Not the Christ They Wanted

## Isaiah 53:1-3; Luke 4:16-30 ESV

Homecoming!

It's the Sabbath—Saturday—and Jesus of Nazareth has come home—to Nazareth. Jesus goes to the synagogue—the village church, and school, and community center and small claims court. Today, it's the place where the men gather for religion—as they do every week—to read God's Word and talk about what it means.

There's Jesus—Jesus Who's been coming to this synagogue and sitting along the wall with His dad—His earthly dad, Joseph—since His thirteenth birthday, the day Jesus became a man in the eyes of the Jewish community in Nazareth. Jesus is all grown up now. He grew up in this very village. He is a man in every way—and has been—for a number of years.

Not long ago, He left town—this town—their town—and started making something of a name for Himself in other towns. What do you know? "Hometown boy makes good"—or something. And here He is back again—back in the synagogue where He grew up.

That's got to be weird!

There's His Little League coach—and His scout master. And there's the guy who taught Jesus geography in school and doubled as their part-time, self-taught rabbi—and beside *him*, all of Joseph's old buddies who used to stop by the carpentry shop and talk things over when Jesus was growing up. And, of course, there are all the boyhood friends of Jesus, now grown men themselves. And Jesus.

Treated like the honored guest—Jesus has been asked to read the holy scriptures and comment on them. If that's not weird, it's going to feel like it is. And it's going to get weirder for the men of Nazareth sitting on the stone benches that run around the walls of their synagogue as this totally familiar Stranger, Jesus, sits down and starts to talk about an age-old prophecy being fulfilled right then and there, right in front of them. It's gotta be a weird experience for everybody.

❧

They recognize the face, but the message stumps them. You think you know Jesus. You grow up with Him or watch Him grow up around you, and you're prepared to let Him impress you, and then one day, He says something or does something that makes it crystal clear that you don't know Jesus nearly as well as you thought you did. You sit there and look at Him and wonder, "What in the world is going on?" And remember, these are the *religious* leaders of His hometown—His Nazareth neighbors—the men who helped raise Him.

But they didn't raise Him like *that*!

Jesus isn't saying what they taught Him to say. He's not acting the way they think He ought to act. He's reading scripture that promises a Messiah from God, and He's telling all these old familiar faces that God is fulfilling that promise—as He speaks!

But Jesus doesn't use the magic words—He doesn't say, "This promise just applies to us." He doesn't tailor His "pitch" to popular expectations. They want a Messiah—a Christ—but *that's* not the one they want.

❧

On the one hand, we know Jesus too well, and on the other, we don't know Him at all. And in the end—or the end of the beginning, at least—those who grew up with Jesus want to get rid of Him. They're ready to take Him out and "terminate" Him—in some spot familiar to all of them, no doubt. And the story of Nazareth—His hometown—becomes the prophecy of His ministry: *"He came to his own…and his own [people] did not receive him."*[82]

Jesus of Nazareth is not the Christ that Nazareth wants.

While Jesus is reading and applying Isaiah for them, is God applying Isaiah to Jesus?

> *"He grew up before him like a tender shoot,*
> *and like a root out of dry ground.*
> *He was despised and rejected by men,*
> *a man of sorrows, and familiar with suffering."*

For saying what He is saying, they grab Jesus and are ready to toss Him off the cliff or stone Him or do something to Him to make His life difficult, if not impossible—His old friends from His old hometown. And no matter how many wonderful words He speaks and no matter how many wondrous works He performs, there will always be those who reject Him and what He says— and want to shut Him up. They were there in Nazareth at the beginning. They will be there outside Jerusalem at the end. And if we are not careful, they will be *us*.

❦

"But we know Jesus!"
And so did they, seemingly.
"But we're His friends!"
So were they, to start with.
"But we would never do Him harm!"
Physically, no; you can't anymore.

---

[82] John 1:11, ESV.

But you can ignore His voice[83] or misinterpret His message to you and to the world. You can sit idly by while others do the dirty work, and then rationalize your actions, or lack thereof.

And because the temptation is always there to do just that, there is Lent, the time between Nazareth and Calvary to humble your heart and turn your attention to what a rejecting world is going to put our Christ through. It is the time God has given us to reflect on the ways we join the mob and try to push Jesus where He has no intention of going. It is that season for taking up crosses—like Him and with Him—and getting familiar with Him in ways His old friends and neighbors in Nazareth never did.

Turns out, Jesus just wasn't the Christ the hometown crowd wanted. But it also turns out that Jesus was the only Christ they or anybody else was going to get. He is the only Christ we've got. It would behoove us, then, to get to know Him better in these days of reflection and sacrificial living ahead.

&#8766;

Do we know Jesus?

Not as well as we could, or should, for our own benefit.

Are we His friends?

We want to be and intend to be, but even our best intentions falter under the weight of our own frailty and foolishness.

Would we do Him harm?

Better we embrace the harm He underwent for us, and bear the sign of His suffering for all the world to see, so that, in humble acknowledgement of our need, we do the Great Physician no harm (by rebellion or spiritual waywardness) that would grieve His Spirit.

*"He was despised and rejected by men,*
*a man of sorrows, and familiar with suffering…"*

…even in Nazareth—in His own hometown.

---

[83] John 10:27.

But not here—not today. In this "synagogue"—in this place where we study and worship and come together in holy fellowship—we honor Jesus and hear His word and know that

> *"He was pierced for our transgressions,*
> *he was crushed for our iniquities;*
> *the punishment that brought us peace was upon him,*
> *and by his wounds we are healed."*

And we know that Jesus of Nazareth is exactly the Christ we want.

ও‑৩

## Luke 4:31-37 RSV

[31] *And [Jesus] went down to Capernaum, a city of Galilee. And he was teaching them on the Sabbath,* [32] *and they were astonished at his teaching, for his word possessed authority.* [33] *And in the synagogue there was a man who had the spirit of an unclean demon, and he cried out with a loud voice,* [34] *"Ha! What have you to do with us, Jesus of Nazareth? Have you come to destroy us? I know who you are—the Holy One of God."* [35] *But Jesus rebuked him, saying, "Be silent and come out of him!" And when the demon had thrown him down in their midst, he came out of him, having done him no harm.* [36] *And they were all amazed and said to one another, "What is this word? For with authority and power he commands the unclean spirits, and they come out!"* [37] *And reports about him went out into every place in the surrounding region.*

&#x2767;

# 8.

# Evil Spirits in Holy Places

## Luke 4:31-37 RSV

There is a statue in St. Peter's Basilica in Rome that is one of the most famous statues in the world. It is certainly the most awe inspiring I've ever seen. The statue, carved out of Carrera marble by Michelangelo, is called *The Pieta*. It depicts the lifeless body of the crucified Christ draped across the lap of His mother, Mary.

*The Pieta* is located in the first chapel, or alcove, on the right as you enter the massive church. It is the most visited spot in the cathedral—after the Tomb of St. Peter—and all who come to see the statue stand before it in silent wonder, stunned by the beauty and power of the portrayal of the sacrifice of the Cross. To be in its presence is to be on holy ground.

And yet, on Pentecost Sunday in 1972, a lunatic walked into St. Peter's with a hammer, climbed over the guard rail and, to the horror of everyone there, began smashing the statue, shouting, "I am Jesus Christ!"

જ્જ

But, of course, this was not the first occasion when *"a man possessed by a demon, an evil spirit"* lashed out at Jesus. Except for the hammer, the same thing happened in the synagogue in Capernaum

53

when Jesus—the Person, not the statue—had an awestruck crowd gathered around Him. The crowd was in their synagogue—their holy place. And Jesus was there, which made it holier still—holier than it had ever been, in fact—holier than they could imagine. And even there—even then—an evil spirit was present—present in that holy place—doing its best to destroy all that was holy about it.

*"Let us alone! What do you want with us, Jesus of Nazareth?"*

"Will somebody get this guy out of here? Where are the ushers?"

*"Have you come to destroy us? I know who you are—the Holy One of God!"*

"This is terrible: a man with an evil spirit disrupting our service—attacking Jesus! Is nothing sacred—even in this holy place? What must Jesus think of us?"

What Jesus must think is that evil spirits get into holy places.

The serpent got into the garden God had created[84]—surely a holy place—and into Adam and Eve, who were made in God's holy image.[85] The dust hadn't settled from God's carving the Ten Commandments on a couple of stone tablets before the children of Israel were "dirty dancing"[86] around their golden calf right there at the foot of Mount Sinai.[87] Foreign conquerors from the Babylonians[88] to the Greeks[89] had desecrated God's Temple in Jerusalem and even Pilate had put the idolatrous images of Rome in that holy place of God.[90]

⊱⊰

---

[84] Genesis 3.

[85] Genesis 1:26-27.

[86] Movie, *Dirty Dancing*, 1987.

[87] Genesis 32:1-20.

[88] 2 Kings 25:8-10.

[89] Under Antiochus IV Epiphanes in 167 BC.

[90] See Isadore Singer and Isaac Broydé, "Pilate, Pontius," *Jewish Encyclopedia*, accessed online at http://jewishencyclopedia.com/articles/12147-pilate-pontius.

And today, the spirit of evil encroaches ever more brazenly in *our* holy places. The hearth and home that God blessed and ordained as the primary place of holiness is seemingly helpless before the daily assaults of computer and television pornography, sadistic violence and cynical, corrupting humor. Institutions of learning once hallowed by holy acts and attitudes have been purged of their sacred dimension, and those who would resist the evil tide are judged guilty as lawbreakers. Secular powers increasingly claim the right to define what is sacred for everyone, often substituting the perverted for the holy. Within the churches and before the altars of our land, sacramental acts have been transformed into sacrilege, as Holy Scripture is hollowed out by clergy co-opted by evil and committed to making God's eternal Word conform to contemporary political agendas.

Is nothing sacred?!

வ—௸

Not to evil. To evil, the sacred is the prime target. Where it can, evil will invade, contaminate and destroy all that is holy.

Evil spirits have gotten into our holy places.

They certainly have, but to call evil "they" is not entirely accurate. As Pogo said, "We have met the enemy, and he is us."[91] Evil spirits get into our holy places because they get into us who go to holy places. *"Know ye not that your body is the temple of the Holy Spirit?"*[92]

Well, some of us still do, but even we are infected by evil spirits, for *"the heart is deceitful above all things, and desperately wicked."*[93] The first person to vandalize *The Pieta*, it happens, was Michelangelo

---

[91] Walt Kelly, "Pogo" Syndicated Comic Strip, April 22, 1971. The line is a "take off" on U.S. Navy Commodore Oliver Hazard Perry's announcement of an American victory over British naval forces in the Battle of Lake Erie during the War of 1812: "We have met the enemy, and they are ours...."

[92] 1 Corinthians 6:19, KJV.

[93] Jeremiah 17:9, KJV.

himself, whose pride was so offended when he heard people saying some other sculptor had probably carved it, that he went back the night it was unveiled and chiseled his name across Mary's sash.[94]

❧

Paul wrote, *"Although I want to do good, evil is right there with me."*[95] Bingo!

Most of us who come to *this* holy place won't make it through a hymn—or a prayer—certainly not a sermon—without the evil spirit in us urging us to think—if not an evil thought—then at least one that is irrelevant or inattentive—something that's nothing in itself, perhaps, but that will clog our ears and close our minds for those important few seconds or minutes when God would otherwise capture our thoughts and kindle our hearts with some revelation that would draw us closer to Him—or answer that nagging spiritual question—or calm that cold, clammy fear.

"What was that? Oh, my mind wandered."

And the opportunity for inspiration is passed—gone. The evil spirit has done its job—again—even in this holy place—*your* holy place. You can understand why Paul would cry out in exasperation, *"O wretched man that I am! who shall deliver me...?"*[96]

Who, indeed!

But we'll come back to that.

❧

Evil spirits don't want any place to be truly holy, and if the evil spirit can't keep you out of holy places, it can at least try to keep the effect of the holy out of you. Even in this place, it will tempt you: "Don't listen. Don't care. Don't believe. Don't submit to that other Spirit—God's Holy Spirit."

---

[94] William E. Wallace, *Life and Early Works (Michelangelo: Selected Scholarship in English)*, 1995, p. 233.
[95] Romans 7:21, NIV.
[96] Romans 7:24, KJV.

But in the synagogue in Capernaum—in their holy place—it is the man with the evil spirit who cries out in exasperation. Jesus is teaching in this synagogue—already astonishing the listeners— already demonstrating His awesome spiritual authority. Why did the evil spirit in the man cry out? Why couldn't the evil spirit just ignore Jesus?

In the movie *A Few Good Men*, there is a dramatic courtroom confrontation between a young Navy lawyer and a corrupt, but cagey, Marine colonel. The heated exchange escalates until, finally, the attorney angrily demands to be told the truth and the colonel on the witness stand yells back, "You can't handle the truth!"[97]

It turns out that the colonel's version of truth is evil. And his evil truth does not serve him well.

Jesus in Capernaum is teaching another truth—divine truth. And the angry outburst that interrupts Jesus reveals that it is evil that can't handle divine truth.[98] Jesus did not come to co-exist with evil, or even to prove that evil could not conquer Him. Jesus came to this world—to holy places—and to places that were anything but—to drive a stake through the heart of evil and kill it forever— to cast it out of every human heart.[99]

When the evil spirit in the man cried out, Jesus recognized it for what it was—who it was. Jesus was no stranger to evil and evil was no stranger to Him. They had met before.[100]

Evil is deceptive, but it is not deceived. Evil knows its Enemy; it knows God—the only power that evil cannot corrupt or conquer. Because the evil spirit knows Who Jesus is, it knows it will have to obey Him if it cannot distract or bluff Him.

ॐ∽ॐ

---

[97] Jack Nicholson's character, Marine Colonel Nathan Jessup, *A Few Good Men*, 1992.
[98] John 1:5.
[99] Galatians 1:4.
[100] Luke 4:1-13.

Of course, evil does not want to let go—to give up control and come out of any heart where it has made itself at home. Evil will have to be cast out. And it will be, because evil cannot withstand the power of God's word.

To be separated from the evil inside can be an ugly and painful process for a time, but peace and health await the man who brought the evil spirit into the holy place. And to the evil spirit, Jesus says, *"Be silent and come out!"*—which the spirit does because it has to.

Wherever Jesus went, every life He touched, He sanctified—if the person would let Him.

Jesus sanctified this world by coming here—by being here and touching the evil of this world with the holiness of heaven. And what Jesus did to the evil spirit in the man in Capernaum, Jesus did to other evil spirits in other places,[101] and eventually to the evil spirit's boss when Jesus came out of His tomb alive on Easter morning. Jesus conquered all evil, once for all.

Oh, evil still tries to be a bother. Evil goes where it can and stirs up as much trouble as it can. And places that have been holy may cease to seem so under evil's influence. But do not be deceived—even by evil spirits in holy places.

Yes, holy places may be invaded by evil spirits, but the good news for us and the very, very bad news for evil is that, with the coming of Jesus Christ, the Holy Spirit is now invading evil places.[102]

స్‍

There are places that evil cannot go—holy places—even today in this remarkably evil world—and certainly now and forever evil cannot go into the infinite realms of heaven. But there is no evil place that the Holy Spirit cannot go—and has not gone—to shine

---

[101] Luke 7:21; 8:2.
[102] Matthew 16:18.

God's searing light of holiness and cast out evil, no matter how deeply entrenched. There is no evil place that cannot be sanctified—hallowed—by the uncontestable power of Him the evil spirit called *"the Holy One of Israel."*

No one was created evil, or to be evil.[103] Evil has become our nature by our individual, if misled, choices.[104] But evil does not have to be anyone's destiny. Evil hardens your heart and muddles your mind. The Holy Spirit heals your heart and clears your mind.[105]

The synagogue in Capernaum was a holy place. And in that holy place—in the presence of Jesus Himself, evil appeared. But Jesus overcame the evil that came into the holy place with a holiness that evil could not withstand.

Does Jesus have the power to cast out the evil spirits that come into the holy places you share with Him? Can Jesus make your home holy? Or your school? Or the place where you work or play? Can He sanctify the places you go in this broken, evil world?

"Who will rescue us? Who will deliver us?" Paul asks in exasperation.

And then, *"Thanks be to God!"* he says.

Who?

*"Jesus Christ our Lord!"*[106]

Jesus did not despair when He met an evil spirit in a holy place. Jesus brought the Holy Spirit into every evil place—as He will for you.

৵৽

---

103 Genesis 1:26-28.
104 Genesis 3:6.
105 Proverbs 28:14; John 12:40.
106 Romans 7:25, ESV.

## Luke 5:1-11 NRSV

*¹ Once while Jesus was standing beside the lake of Gennesaret, and the crowd was pressing in on him to hear the word of God, ² he saw two boats there at the shore of the lake; the fishermen had gone out of them and were washing their nets. ³ He got into one of the boats, the one belonging to Simon, and asked him to put out a little way from the shore. Then he sat down and taught the crowds from the boat. ⁴ When he had finished speaking, he said to Simon, "Put out into the deep water and let down your nets for a catch." ⁵ Simon answered, "Master, we have worked all night long but have caught nothing. Yet if you say so, I will let down the nets." ⁶ When they had done this, they caught so many fish that their nets were beginning to break. ⁷ So they signaled their partners in the other boat to come and help them. And they came and filled both boats, so that they began to sink. ⁸ But when Simon Peter saw it, he fell down at Jesus' knees, saying, "Go away from me, Lord, for I am a sinful man!" ⁹ For he and all who were with him were amazed at the catch of fish that they had taken; ¹⁰ and so also were James and John, sons of Zebedee, who were partners with Simon. Then Jesus said to Simon, "Do not be afraid; from now on you will be catching people." ¹¹ When they had brought their boats to shore, they left everything and followed him.*

ॐ-ॐ

# 9.

# Jesus in Your Boat

## Luke 5:1-11 NRSV

Isn't it amazing? You can be doing anything, and Jesus will come along. Simon Peter was cleaning his nets; he'd been fishing all night. And Jesus came along.

But He didn't just come along—He got into Peter's boat—and into his life.

What were you doing when Jesus came along? Working? Attending to important matters? Getting ready for the future? Trying to get some rest or forgetting about some disappointment and getting on with your life?

Jesus is always about the business for which God the Father sent Him. Jesus is always telling the Good News—always offering hope and forgiveness, redemption and salvation. And sometimes, He comes along and gets in your "boat." Sometimes Jesus turns up while you're doing something else and says, "Help Me out here a little bit. I want to talk to people and I want you to help Me do so. Maneuver Me into position."

And you have to interrupt what you're doing—set your other work and plans aside and get Jesus in a position where He can talk to people and they can hear Him. Peter did it; so can you.

And then, after you push Jesus off the safe and solid ground, out a little bit—after you get comfortable and familiar with the small tasks—the simple tasks of obedience—when Jesus is done with that, He will say: *"Put out into the deep water."*

Now that's a problem if you're trying to keep your relationship with Jesus small and simple—comfortable and manageable. Things are easy in the shallow water, but Jesus isn't a shallow water guy: *"Put out into the deep water."*

Jesus is in Peter's boat and if Peter goes out into the deep water with Jesus, everything else will be put on hold until they get back. Peter will have to pay more attention to what's going on in the boat. He will be less distracted by what's on the shore. He will be more available to Jesus and, probably, more attentive to Him.

And why does Jesus want to take Peter into deeper water?

Jesus is going to give Peter things to do that Peter has tried on his own to do and failed. Jesus is going to tell Peter to do things that will demonstrate the power of God—things that can't be explained any other way. Jesus is going to tell Peter things in the deep water that will make no sense to Peter—that Peter will have to take on faith—believe in faith—and obey.

"Peter, let down your nets and catch fish."

"I tried that," Peter says, "and caught nothing. But because You tell me to, I will do it again."

Peter doesn't have much faith, but he is obedient. And that is enough—for now.

Peter is out in the deep water with Jesus, and Peter does what Jesus tells him to, and he catches fish like he has never caught them before.

Peter is impressed. Truth be told: He's scared out of his wits! In the deep water, things happen that Peter can't explain—except to say that Jesus is in them and something's in Jesus that's like nothing else in this world.

But, of course, Jesus didn't get into Peter's boat just to do impressive things. The miraculous catch was not the point—it was merely the illustration of the point: "I can enable you to catch fish, which is your goal—and catch more than you could ever imagine.

"My goal is that you catch men—reel in people who are over their heads in deep water—and rescue them from drowning in their sins. My goal for you is that you fish more men out of hell than you could ever imagine."

Peter went out into the deep water with Jesus and Jesus changed his life. And when they got back, Peter left what he had been doing, because now he had something better to do—something Jesus gave him to do while they were out there together in the deep water.

Peter's was not—is not—the only boat Jesus gets into. Jesus climbs into a lot of boats to do the Father's work.

Where is yours? Tied up securely on shore while you attend to other things? Floating safely in the shallows while Jesus attends to other people? Moving out into deep waters and deeper wonders? Left so you can follow Jesus and share in the greatest catch of all?

Peter was the first disciple—the first to follow Jesus. His experience is the example for all of us. Discipleship is a scary business. But remember what Jesus said: "Do not be afraid. From now on you will be catching—rescuing—people."

৯৽৽৻

## Luke 7:36-47 NRSV

[36] *One of the Pharisees asked Jesus to eat with him, and he went into the Pharisee's house and took his place at the table.*

[37] *And a woman in the city, who was a sinner, having learned that he was eating in the Pharisee's house, brought an alabaster jar of ointment.* [38] *She stood behind him at his feet, weeping, and began to bathe his feet with her tears and to dry them with her hair. Then she continued kissing his feet and anointing them with the ointment.*

[39] *Now when the Pharisee who had invited him saw it, he said to himself, "If this man were a prophet, he would have known who and what kind of woman this is who is touching him—that she is a sinner."*

[40] *Jesus spoke up and said to him, "Simon, I have something to say to you."*

*"Teacher," he replied, "speak."*

[41] *"A certain creditor had two debtors; one owed five hundred denarii, and the other fifty.* [42] *When they could not pay, he canceled the debts for both of them. Now which of them will love him more?"*

[43] *Simon answered, "I suppose the one for whom he canceled the greater debt."*

*And Jesus said to him, "You have judged rightly."* [44] *Then turning toward the woman, he said to Simon, "Do you see this woman? I entered your house; you gave me no water for my feet, but she has bathed my feet with her tears and dried them with her hair.* [45] *You gave me no kiss, but from the time I came in she has not stopped kissing my feet.* [46] *You did not anoint my head with oil, but she has anointed my feet with ointment.* [47] *Therefore, I tell you, her sins, which were many, have been forgiven; hence she has shown great love. But the one to whom little is forgiven, loves little."*

[48] *Then he said to her, "Your sins are forgiven."*

෨᎒Ꮾ

# 10.

# Debtors Forgiven

## Luke 7:36-47 NRSV

Every week in the *Pilot*—our local newspaper—you can see pictures of people having fun at this party or that. The paper sends photographers out to all the big "doings" so that those of us who are not part of the party can at least see who is and what they are up to.

In the world of Jesus, they did you one better. Since they had no cameras or newspapers—and you had no television—you could go and watch the parties in your neighborhood or village in "real time."

Those not invited as guests were welcome to peek in the open windows or come in and line up along the walls to see what those who had been invited were wearing and eating, and to listen to their conversation around the table. This week, the party—a formal dinner party—is at Simon's house.

Now, this is not Simon Peter the Apostle; it's another Simon—a Pharisee—and a fellow affluent enough to host a dinner for a visiting Rabbi named Jesus—and religious enough to want to.

Jesus has come to town—preceded, no doubt, by His reputation as a powerful Preacher and a possible Prophet. The report on Him will include the assertion that He associates—even eats—with tax collectors and other sinners.

The townsfolk hear this Jesus preach and see that He certainly does seem to have an openness to everyone, however sordid one's reputation. He has preached the gospel: grace for all—forgiveness, redemption, reconciliation with God—no matter what you have done in the past. The townsfolk are impressed with Jesus and what He has to say. Two of them are so impressed that they respond with dramatic action.

One of these is Simon the Pharisee, who invites Jesus to be the Guest of honor at a banquet in his home. The other person, a woman who seems completely unlike Simon in every way, also responds to Jesus—but that will "keep" for a moment.

First, we need to go to Simon's house and join the crowd of uninvited guests observing the festivities. Everybody there knows what should happen. The protocols of politeness in such situations are clearly defined and well established. They know what to expect, but nothing goes as expected—not even for Simon, who's hosting the party.

Have you ever put on a big party only to have it blow up in your face? When a party fails, it's usually the food—or the weather. It could be that an important guest doesn't show up or that the people or the conversations are just boring.

At Simon's party, the food is fine and the weather is wonderful. The Guest of honor has shown up on time and the conversation is riveting. Simon's party blows up in his face because he tries to flip the conventions of courtesy upside down. He has designed an evening, not to honor Jesus as a prophet, but to expose Him as a fraud, subjecting Jesus and His gospel to public humiliation and shame.

Simon intended to "ambush" his Guest of honor, but his social booby-trap backfires. It backfires because his Target turns out to be a Prophet after all—a true Prophet and more.

Simon planned to show Jesus such disrespect in front of the fine folks of the village that Jesus would get up and leave in a resentful huff. But Jesus doesn't budge. What Simon didn't realize was that the Man of Sorrows Who would quietly endure the Cross could—and would—easily endure Simon's calculated insults to His dignity.

స్త్రోం

But Jesus does more than endure the scorn; He confronts it—though it is unheard of for a guest to criticize his host's hospitality. Jesus confronts Simon's behavior—firmly, but without malice.

Common courtesy required a host to provide water for a guest to wash his feet upon entering the house. The feet of an honored guest would have been washed by a servant—or in special cases—by the son of the host.

*"I entered your house,"* says Jesus (and He might have added, "as *your* invited Guest of honor"), *"but you gave me no water for my feet."*

Common courtesy required that a host greet a guest with a kiss on each cheek. A respected religious teacher would have been kissed on the hand by the host and all his sons.

Jesus tells Simon simply, *"You gave me no kiss."*

Common courtesy called for a host to anoint his guest's head with olive oil.

"You did not do this," Jesus points out.

And you will notice that the party is definitely not going as Simon had planned.

Simon had planned to leave Jesus sputtering in ridiculed rage. Instead, Simon has been reduced to silent and public shame—in his own house—before his friends and all the "viewers" of the village—among whom is the woman I mentioned earlier.

That woman heard Jesus preach, and what He said about the love and grace of God made such an impact on her that she wanted to show Jesus what she thought of Him, too.

Simon invited Jesus to dinner and planned to humiliate Him. This woman—who is apparently well known in town as a "bad woman"—planned to honor Jesus and went to Simon's house for that purpose. Maybe she went to Simon's house because Simon was also well known in the village. Maybe what she knew of Simon's reputation made her worry when she heard that he had invited Jesus to his home.

Either way, while Simon proposed to withhold honor; she proposed to bestow it. She brought her expensive perfume—perhaps a necessity in the "line of business" she had been led by Jesus to get out of. The perfume was probably the only physical thing of value she had—and she brought it in its alabaster jar to pour out upon the feet of Jesus as an offering of gratitude and godly love. And she positioned herself in the audience behind Jesus for this purpose.

Simon has seen her behind Jesus, as he studied his intended Target. And Simon knows who she is—she has a reputation in town. Simon is delighted that Jesus does not recoil from the woman—as Simon thinks any godly man should do. And Simon, no doubt, sees his plan exceeding his expectations when the woman breaks down and weeps a torrent of tears that fall upon Jesus' feet. Then she violates all propriety by letting her hair down in public before all these men, to dry her tears from Jesus' feet.

"That proves it!" Simon thinks. "No prophet would let a woman like that do a thing like that."

Game, set and match!

કે-ક

And that's when Simon learns that Jesus doesn't play by the rules of the world. Basking in smug satisfaction, Simon may be surprised that Jesus can even muster the self-control to speak. But speak Jesus does, and the voice Simon hears is disturbingly calm and collected, *"Simon, I have something to say to you."*

You know what Jesus is going to say; you heard it just a moment ago. But before Jesus "takes Simon down to parade rest,"[107] Jesus tells him a story—a parable. It's barely a story—more like a scene: Two people owed somebody money. One owed a lot; the other, not so much. Neither could pay his debt and the somebody they owed forgave both of their debts in full.

End of story.

❧

It's the end of the parable, but not the end of its purpose. There's still the matter of love.

There's debt. There's forgiveness. And there's love.

In Simon's mind, a prophet should be able to recognize a sinner. And Simon doesn't think Jesus is a prophet because Jesus doesn't seem to recognize someone Simon sees as the biggest sinner in town.

But the truth is that Jesus does have the prophet's ability to recognize sinners. He has recognized not one, but two. Jesus knows that the woman is a sinner—that her behavior has created a debt—to God and her community—that she can never overcome.

She is a genuine debtor—whose debt has been forgiven in full. God has taken the weight of that debt off the ledger—and off her heart. Her heart is now free to love God and the One Who announced her forgiveness to her. Her deeds demonstrate her love. Jesus knows she is a sinner, but He isn't worried about her. She has received the forgiveness of her debt.

❧

---

[107] Like a drill sergeant publicly chewing out a new recruit who's messed up.

It is the other sinner that concerns Jesus—the debtor who does not acknowledge his debt and, therefore, sees no need for the debt to be forgiven. Jesus is more than a prophet; He knows what's in the mind of men. He knew what was going on in Simon's mind—and heart—even as Simon invited Him home.

So why did Jesus go? Why did He subject Himself to Simon's assault on His dignity?

Because Simon owes a debt Simon cannot repay—and Simon will not admit it. Simon has been forgiven his debt, but he sees no need to accept the grace that God has given him.

Jesus went to Simon's house for the same reason He will go to the house of Zacchaeus, one of those dirty tax collectors Pharisees like Simon despise so much: Jesus *"came to seek and to save the lost."*[108] Jesus will eat with sinners in order to save sinners—to tell them—convince them—that their un-payable debt has been paid in full.

And how does Jesus know when His job is done—in Simon's house or Zacchaeus'?

The giveaway is when the debtor believes that God has forgiven his debt—and loves God accordingly. Forgiven debtors love the One Who has forgiven their debts.[109]

So how about you?

The woman thought her debt was too big to ever be forgiven, until Jesus set her straight. Simon thought he didn't have any debt that needed forgiving, until Jesus set him straight.

No debt too large—no debt too small. All debts must—and can—be forgiven.

What about your debts?

Yes, *your* debts! Your debts have been forgiven—forgiven in full.

Don't you just love it? Don't you just love Him? Don't you?

෨෴෨

---

[108] Luke 19:10, ESV.
[109] Luke 19:8-9.

## Luke 7:36-50 ESV

In the Jewish culture of Jesus' day, to invite someone to share your table was to express great honor and esteem for the guest. But Jesus was invited to a dinner by a host who intended to humiliate Him in front of the whole town.

What the Pharisee had not foreseen was that, first, a forgiven woman, and then Jesus Himself, would turn the tables and reveal to all the evil intent of the host who held himself above Jesus and a woman who showed Jesus true honor.

❧

*[36] One of the Pharisees asked [Jesus] to eat with him, and he went into the Pharisee's house and reclined at table. [37] And behold, a woman of the city, who was a sinner, when she learned that he was reclining at table in the Pharisee's house, brought an alabaster flask of ointment, [38] and standing behind him at his feet, weeping, she began to wet his feet with her tears and wiped them with the hair of her head and kissed his feet and anointed them with the ointment. [39] Now when the Pharisee who had invited him saw this, he said to himself, "If this man were a prophet, he would have known who and what sort of woman this is who is touching him, for she is a sinner." [40] And Jesus answering said to him, "Simon, I have something to say to you." And he answered, "Say it, Teacher."*

*[41] "A certain moneylender had two debtors. One owed five hundred denarii, and the other fifty. [42] When they could not pay, he cancelled the debt of both. Now which of them will love him more?" [43] Simon answered, "The one, I suppose, for whom he cancelled the larger debt." And he said to him, "You have judged rightly." [44] Then turning toward the woman he said to Simon, "Do you see this woman? I entered your house; you gave me no water for my feet, but she has wet my feet with her tears and wiped them with her hair. [45] You gave me no kiss, but from the time I came in she has not ceased to kiss my feet. [46] You did not anoint my head with oil, but she has anointed my feet with ointment. [47] Therefore I tell you, her sins, which are many, are forgiven—for she loved much. But he who is forgiven little, loves little."*

 [48] *And he said to her, "Your sins are forgiven." [49] Then those who were at table with him began to say among themselves, "Who is this, who even forgives sins?" [50] And he said to the woman, "Your faith has saved you; go in peace."*

ॐ✶

# 11.

# Tables Turned

## Luke 7:36-50 ESV

Listening to the story you heard earlier about the dinner party at the Pharisee's house is kind of like watching a cricket match: Unless you know the rules, you'll never understand the game, even when they're playing it right in front of you.

The rules you don't know, in this case, are the rules of etiquette and hospitality in the ancient Middle East, many of which are still practiced—religiously—even today. Not here, of course, but there. And you won't be able to understand what's happening in the Pharisee's house if you don't understand what's *supposed* to happen but doesn't. So let's review the rules—that everybody *there* knew by heart—that we don't know at all.

To invite someone to be a guest in your home—to invite that someone to "recline at your table" (which was the term used to describe how a formal dinner was eaten because guests were arranged by relative importance on couches around a low table covered with food)—was to show that someone great honor. And the honor involved not just inviting the individual, but the respectful treatment he would receive when he arrived at your house.

The rules of Middle Eastern etiquette required that the invited guest be greeted with a kiss by the host at the door when he arrived. If the guest were a rabbi or religious leader, the host and all his sons would kiss the great man's hand as a sign of even greater respect.

When the guest took his place on his assigned couch, propped on his left elbow with his head toward the table and his feet away from it, a servant would bring a basin of water and a towel and wash his feet. The host would pour olive oil over his guest's head to anoint him as a noble person—a further honor.

And all of this would be very public and ceremonial, because the rule was that formal dinner parties were free entertainments for the community. The doors and the windows of the house were thrown open so that any and all who wished to could come and watch, provided they position themselves out of the way, behind the feet of the reclining guests.

One member of the public in particular has taken advantage of the opportunity to observe at this one particular party by positioning herself right behind Jesus. The translation you heard earlier introducing her says she was "a woman in that town who lived a sinful life." That wording is really too charitable. The original language labels her more harshly—the way all her neighbors did: "*sinner.*"

She was the well-known, sinful woman in town. And yet she shows up at Simon's house—a Pharisee's house—to see Jesus honored. Simon sees her and knows immediately who she is, and under normal circumstances, would have avoided her like the plague. But at the moment, he's hosting a dinner party—of sorts.

She sees Simon—and what he's doing by what he is *not* doing as the host—and she is appalled.

Jesus sees them both—and knows that sinners come in many different forms.

So, let the games begin.

❧·❧

And the game Simon the Pharisee is playing is a version of "Turn the Tables." He has invited Jesus to be the Guest of honor at a formal dinner—presumably because Jesus has just preached the good news of God's redemption in the town—a powerful sermon of forgiveness and grace, if the reaction of the sinful woman is any indication.

But Simon didn't react to the sermon the way the woman did, apparently—because his purpose in getting Jesus to recline at his table is to turn the tables on Jesus by showering Jesus, not with praise and honor, but with public humiliation.

The Pharisee, who makes it his life's work to enforce the rules on everybody else, studiously breaks the rules himself in order to subject Jesus to shame and ridicule. He does not kiss Jesus when He arrives. He does not have anyone wash Jesus' feet. He does not anoint the head of his invited Guest with oil.

And all this he does—or does *not* do—in front of an awestruck audience of onlookers.

At some point in this parade of public insults (Simon assumes) Jesus will blow His top and storm out with His dignity in tatters. What else would you do when you realize you've been socially bushwhacked?

છે⚬⚬ई

But Jesus says nothing—does nothing. He endures the insults. His dignity is of no importance compared to what He came to Simon's house to accomplish. Jesus has some table turning of another sort to do.

But before Jesus can respond to Simon's breathtaking slights, the woman standing behind Jesus does some table turning of her own. You see, hospitality in the Middle Eastern village is a community responsibility. The signals Simon is sending Jesus reflect on the whole town, and his message to Jesus is the last thing the woman wants said to the Teacher Who just hours before had taught her that even she is forgiven by God.

She brought the most valuable thing she has—her alabaster jar of perfume—which she won't be using anymore, by the way—to give it to Jesus in gratitude for the grace of God He has promised her.

But she is not prepared for Simon's terrible treatment of Jesus in front of everybody. And she begins to cry in helpless anger and pain, her tears falling on the feet that Simon had no one wash. Seeing and seizing the opportunity to show this humble sign of hospitality, she lets down her hair to be the towel Simon would surely not give her for drying these holy feet, voluntarily humiliating herself to mitigate the humiliation to which Simon has been subjecting Jesus, redeeming the honor of the Man Who had brought redemption to her.

And then this woman, so accustomed to kissing men in lust, now kisses the feet of Jesus in a different kind of love, a sacrificial substitute for the sign of welcome Simon had withheld.

And the perfume that was to be a gift of gratitude, now becomes a holy offering, a greater prize than household oil, poured out as an anointing of the Son of David sent to be her Savior.

Simon has had his "at bats," and the woman has had hers, and the spectators around the room are no doubt stunned by the play of both. But the next inning—or whatever they call a round of cricket—belongs to Jesus.

☙❦

But before the Master makes His move, we learn a little more about Simon.

Simon the Pharisee, the rule keeper, is called for intentionally breaking the rules, but he doesn't care about that right now. Instead of acknowledging his dirty play, he wants to question the woman's qualifications to be an umpire: "She doesn't have a right to throw a penalty flag! She doesn't even have a right to play the game!"

Simon should not have tried to turn the tables on Jesus, and he should never play poker with his Guest. Jesus reads his inner thoughts on his judgmental face and calls him on it.

Jesus looks at the woman, but speaks to His increasingly uncomfortable host: "You broke the rule about greeting your guest with respect. This woman made up for your failure. You broke the rule about washing a guest's feet. This woman made up for your failure. You broke the rule about anointing a guest. This woman made up for that failure, too, and at much greater cost to her than doing what you *should* have done would have cost you."

But even before that, Jesus told Simon—and everybody else— a little story about two debtors forgiven and the level of love that resulted in each. And in telling the story, Jesus turned the tables on Simon and on the woman and on anyone willing to see the truth.

For Simon, people like this woman were simply "sinners," and always would be—while Pharisees like himself were *not* sinners, and never *could* be. What Jesus was saying turned the tables on that pat approach to life, which made Simon determined to turn the tables on Jesus.

But Simon was out of his league, because, in Jesus, God was turning the tables on the whole world of sin—and the devil behind it. Everybody was forgiven—the "big" sinners everybody knew about, and the "little" sinners, too, who acted like they weren't sinners at all and had most people believing them.

"Big" sinners like this unnamed woman were overjoyed at the news, because forgiveness meant there was now a place for them "at the table." The problem came for the "little" sinners like Simon. The "little" sinners—as Simon saw himself, even if that wasn't how *God* saw him—weren't going to be able to pretend any more that they *weren't* sinners.

To receive God's forgiveness, they were going to have to 'fess up,' repent and be redeemed, just like all the "big" sinners they liked to look down on. Simon was going to have to make room at the table for all the sinners who had been forgiven. And he was going to have to repent and be forgiven himself, if he was even to preserve a place at the table for himself.

And so Jesus tells the woman that her sins are forgiven, as He must have told her earlier that day. And now He tells everybody there—all her rejecting neighbors—the same thing about her.

The other guests—all "little" sinners, no doubt—are wondering Who Jesus is that He can forgive sins. Simon knows now that Jesus is the One Who exposes sin as well as forgives it.

They all better figure it out because Jesus has turned the tables. Now *He* is the One Who invites people—sinners—to *His* table.

Sinners—debtors to God, big and small—are forgiven, if they will accept it. Your sins are forgiven, if you will accept it. And a place at the table—His table—is prepared for you.

All the forgiven sinners are crowded around it, but there's still room for you. "The table of the Lord is set before you, let all who desire"—all of us forgiven sinners—"...come...."[110]

❧

---

[110] From the Communion Liturgy in *The Episcopal Book of Common Prayer*, 1928.

## Luke 8:26-39 NRSV

*26 Then they arrived at the country of the Gerasenes, which is opposite Galilee. 27 As [Jesus] stepped out on land, a man of the city who had demons met him. For a long time he had worn no clothes, and he did not live in a house but in the tombs.*

*28 When he saw Jesus, he fell down before him and shouted at the top of his voice, "What have you to do with me, Jesus, Son of the Most High God? I beg you, do not torment me"— 29 for Jesus had commanded the unclean spirit to come out of the man. (For many times it had seized him; he was kept under guard and bound with chains and shackles, but he would break the bonds and be driven by the demon into the wilds.)*

*30 Jesus then asked him, "What is your name?"*

*He said, "Legion"; for many demons had entered him. 31 They begged him not to order them to go back into the abyss.*

*32 Now there on the hillside a large herd of swine was feeding; and the demons begged Jesus to let them enter these. So he gave them permission.*

*33 Then the demons came out of the man and entered the swine, and the herd rushed down the steep bank into the lake and was drowned.*

*34 When the swineherds saw what had happened, they ran off and told it in the city and in the country. 35 Then people came out to see what had happened, and when they came to Jesus, they found the man from whom the demons had gone sitting at the feet of Jesus, clothed and in his right mind. And they were afraid. 36 Those who had seen it told them how the one who had been possessed by demons had been healed.*

*37 Then all the people of the surrounding country of the Gerasenes asked Jesus to leave them; for they were seized with great fear. So he got into the boat and returned.*

*38 The man from whom the demons had gone begged that he might be with him; but Jesus sent him away, saying, 39 "Return to your home, and declare how much God has done for you."*

*So he went away, proclaiming throughout the city how much Jesus had done for him.*

❦

# 12.

# Cured

## Luke 8:26-39 NRSV

It's a colorful and captivating story we just heard: A crazy man confronts Jesus and Jesus directs the demons that drove the man crazy into a bunch of pigs that run off a cliff and drown. But don't get distracted; it's not about the pigs. It's about the man who was healed—and the One Who put him back in his right mind.

Focus on the man. He's become something that is barely a man at all. Here is a man who is cut off from everybody—even himself. He won't wear clothes. He camps out in the cemetery. He's been in and out of custody more times than you can count. His life is out of control.

And then Jesus arrives. The wild man is drawn to Jesus and yet fears what Jesus can do to him—or for him. Inside, he is a man at war with himself; he calls himself "Legion"—army. And isn't it interesting that he is not concerned about the torment his demons are inflicting on him. He wants *Jesus* to leave him alone.

"Don't mess with my demons, Jesus! I've got them right where they want me."

But Jesus will not leave the man—or his demons—alone. Jesus will do battle with the legion of demons who are "dug in" in the life of this man.

Yes, there will be collateral damage, but when Jesus is done, the crazy man will be sitting calmly at His feet, clothed and in his right mind. And "the word on the street" will be, *"The one who had been possessed…has been healed."*

Now look at this: Jesus gives the man back his life and the man wants to spend it with Jesus—which is as it should be. But then Jesus says something you would not expect: "Go home and tell them what God has done for you."

This was a man who didn't—couldn't—live in a house; he lived in the graveyard. But he does have a home. He is a man and so he is almost certainly a husband and probably a father. He has a family, but the demons in his life had cut him off from his family. He lived alone, if you call it "living."

His demons had his life, but Jesus drove the demons out and gave this man his life back. Jesus got him thinking right and now will have him live his life right.

"O Jesus, I want to go wherever You go!"

"No." says Jesus, "Go home to your wife and kids. Be a husband and father who witnesses to your family—who tells them all that God has done for you."

The "legion" of demons has been defeated by the Lord of hosts, and the one who was out of control is now obedient to Jesus. And this man-in-his-right-mind goes not merely to his family with his good news, but to other relatives and to neighbors. He's "all-over-town," telling people what they already know: that Jesus turned his life around.

Jesus turned it inside out and then back again, driving out the man's demons and delivering the Holy Spirit to take their place. Jesus gives him back his life and his home and his family.

There are too many men today who are cut off from their families by the army of demons controlling their lives. The demons say, "Go it alone. Strip yourself of decency and responsibility and any vestige of healthy relationships. Be your own person. Pursue your own goals at the expense of everything else. And don't let anything get in your way." It's lunacy, of course, sheer madness. But oh-so-many are listening.

Thank God that Jesus can heal a man possessed by any demon—and any number of demons. Jesus can put a man back in his right mind and do so many good things for him that he just has to tell somebody. And the place to start telling is at home. A man in his right mind will tell his family all that God has done for him—and he won't stop there.

What has God done for you since Jesus arrived in your life? And whom are you telling?

∂∾⊙

## Luke 9:28-36 NRSV

[28] *Now about eight days after these sayings Jesus took with him Peter and John and James, and went up on the mountain to pray.* [29] *And while he was praying, the appearance of his face changed, and his clothes became dazzling white.* [30] *Suddenly they saw two men, Moses and Elijah, talking to him.* [31] *They appeared in glory and were speaking of his departure, which he was about to accomplish at Jerusalem.* [32] *Now Peter and his companions were weighed down with sleep; but since they had stayed awake, they saw his glory and the two men who stood with him.* [33] *Just as they were leaving him, Peter said to Jesus, "Master, it is good for us to be here; let us make three dwellings, one for you, one for Moses, and one for Elijah"—not knowing what he said.* [34] *While he was saying this, a cloud came and overshadowed them; and they were terrified as they entered the cloud.* [35] *Then from the cloud came a voice that said, "This is my Son, my Chosen; listen to him!"* [36] *When the voice had spoken, Jesus was found alone. And they kept silent and in those days told no one any of the things they had seen.*

இ௸ை

# 13.

# And As He Was Praying...

## Luke 9:28-36 NRSV

Those of you who are reading the Bible through this year have already seen the Transfiguration of Jesus in Matthew's Gospel. This morning, we heard Luke's account. Both Matthew and Luke draw on Mark's Gospel for the basic details: Jesus goes up on a mountain—probably Mount Hermon in the Golan Heights—to pray. It is apparently evening. He takes Peter, James and John with Him and they fall asleep (as they will do again later when He goes to the Garden of Gethsemane outside Jerusalem to pray—on the night before His Crucifixion).[111]

But for now, Jesus is in Galilee, in the north country. At the end of this particular day, Jesus goes up the mountain to pray. We don't know what kind of day Jesus has had before He starts up the mountain. We don't know what His week has been like. We don't know whether He has gone up that mountain every day or whether this is the first time He has been able to break away and hike up to its higher elevations for privacy and perspective.

---

[111] Matthew 26:36-46.

We do know that Jesus prays—frequently, extensively, intensely, and confidently—publicly and privately.[112] And we know that things happen when Jesus prays—miraculous things.[113] Tonight on the mountain will be no exception.

But it will be different.

❧

We are used to Jesus praying and seeing things change—seeing people change. Jesus prays, and fish and loaves are multiplied.[114] Jesus prays, and sick people are healed.[115] But tonight—on the Mount of Transfiguration—Jesus will be praying, and as He is praying, it is Jesus Who will be changed.

Does the idea of prayer changing Jesus startle you?

Much as we would like to deny it, it is very easy to take Jesus for granted—at least in the sense that each of us has a mental image of Who Jesus is. And that image doesn't change much. And if it does change—say because we learn more about Jesus from reading our Bibles or by attending a Sunday School class—the change is really more about us correcting our misconceptions by getting our facts right than about seeing Jesus Himself change.

Even the disciples—walking and talking with Him each day and watching Him work wonders—even these disciples quickly came to think they knew what they were dealing with in Jesus—so much so that they were comfortable nodding off while He prayed nearby.

But this time, Jesus goes up the mountain to pray and, in the process, something incredible happens to Jesus. Jesus is transfigured—in a sense, transformed. Jesus makes contact with a Power that lights Him up like a neon sign on payday. His clothes look like the dazzling white of new snow sparkling in the early

---

112 Matthew 14:23; Mark 1:35; 6:46.
113 John 11:41-44.
114 Matthew 14:19-21.
115 Mark 7:32-35.

morning sun. There is glory all around Him—divine glory—a *shekinah*-on-the-mountain-and-in-the-cloud-where-God-is kind of glory. And Jesus is not the only figure on the mountain bathed in this glory.

When they hang Him on a cross on the hill called Calvary, they will flank Jesus with two criminals.[116] But tonight, on the Mount of Transfiguration, the figures on His left and right are heaven's personifications of the Law and the Prophets: Moses and Elijah.

Moses the Lawgiver and Elijah the fearless voice of God come back to earth from the realms of glory, and yet they stand illuminated in the reflected glory of Jesus, the One Who will complete and fulfill everything they contributed and represent in the plan and purpose of God.

৯৵৶

It's enough to wake the dead, or at least the disciples who are "dead to the world" while the Savior of the world is over there deep in prayer. And they do wake up—Peter, James and John—and wonder what in the world they are seeing.

What do you say—what do you do—when you look up and see Moses and Elijah looking right back at you? What do you do when the Jesus you've become so accustomed to isn't what you're accustomed to at all?

Well, the three no-longer-drowsy disciples don't ask for autographs and they don't pull out their cell phone cameras. Still, Peter's idea of setting up little shrines is pretty lame, as the Gospel writers indicate.

But before Peter can come up with something better, Moses and Elijah are gone, and the light of God's glory is shrouded in the cloud of God's mystery. The content of their conversation with Jesus is superseded by the voice of God Himself, affirming Jesus

---

[116] Luke 23:32-33.

and confirming His understanding of the life purpose to which He has committed Himself.

And then it's over.

Moses and Elijah?

Gone.

Glorious Light?

Gone.

Holy Cloud?

Gone.

Heavenly Voice?

Quiet.

There is only Jesus, Who looks now as He did before they came up the mountain—and Peter, James and John, who don't know what to say, but know that nothing, including and especially Jesus, is what or Who they thought.

Peter, James and John, we can understand. They're like us. You go to pray and you're just as likely to fall asleep. You start out following in the footsteps of Jesus and before you realize it, your mind has wandered, and you have no idea where Jesus is. You spend time with Jesus and before long you think you know all you need to know about Him—all there is to know.

And then, all of a sudden, you wake up and see a Jesus you don't recognize—a Jesus radiating the glory of God—and you don't have a clue what to do in response.

❧

We can come back to that—but what about Jesus? What's going on with Him? Why is He transfigured? What does it mean for Him?

Jesus, we're not. But we need to understand as much as we can about Him because He's the One we're depending on.

All this takes place while Jesus is praying—while He is focused on God and listening to God and grappling with God's will for Him. And because Jesus has been praying—this night and every night—and every day as well—praying, as it were, without ceasing[117]—that divine will for Him—that life purpose put there by God—has become clearer and clearer.

It is a life purpose that will lead unavoidably to death on the Cross.[118] It is a divine will that will require suffering and sacrifice all along the way. It is a contradiction in the most basic human sense—a paradox of divine proportions: To save your life is to lose it; to give up your life is to save it;[119] and all those who believe they will be saved by His sacrifice of His life, will.[120]

And Jesus says "Yes" to God. Jesus turns His face toward Jerusalem[121] and the atoning death that awaits Him there. Jesus teaches His disciples that He is going to give Himself up to those who will crucify Him[122] and that we are to take up our crosses (face up to the hostility our commitment to Him will evoke from the world) and follow Him straight into that opposition.[123]

This life at cross-purposes with the world is not something any sane person would want to undertake if it weren't absolutely necessary, and so God determined that Jesus—and the disciples of Jesus—would know that it *is*. It is—absolutely necessary.

The glory that God shown on Jesus—the Old Testament giants God sent to talk with Jesus and encourage Jesus and strengthen Jesus—the divine words God spoke to claim Jesus and reaffirm the authority and identity of Jesus as God's Son, all send the message that Jesus is infinitely more than we see or have allowed ourselves to believe.

As Jesus is praying, God takes a hidden truth and makes it visible—if only for a brief time before a small group of already

---

[117] 1 Thessalonians 5:17.
[118] Philippians 2:8; 1 John 4:9-10.
[119] Luke 9:24.
[120] Romans 10:9.
[121] Luke 9:51.
[122] Matthew 16:21.
[123] Luke 9:23.

discredited witnesses. But every time Jesus prays, He gives God everything He has and everything God needs to work His will.

What do Peter, James and John see when their Jesus is transfigured before them?

They see for a moment what they will see permanently in the Resurrection.

As Jesus is praying, God is hearing and responding, equipping and blessing. As Jesus is praying, God is providing every resource Jesus will need to succeed in His divinely assigned mission. As Jesus is praying, God is revealing the glory of His Son Who emptied Himself of His own divine prerogatives in order to give Himself fully and finally to God and His service, regardless the cost.[124]

What do you do when you wake up and see a Jesus like you've never seen before?

You don't try to pin Him down or put Him in a tent, however well-intentioned you mean to be—however lovely the shrine you would shut Him up in.

God intends His Son our Savior to be on the move—dynamic. God intends that His Son's disciples will be on the move with Him.

Where is Jesus going?

To Jerusalem. To the Cross. To the grave. To the right hand of the Father in glory,[125] the same glory God clothed Jesus in, one night as He was praying.

Peter and his buddies didn't understand what they saw and heard that night on the mountain—until they saw it and heard it again, as the light rose on Easter morning[126] and as Jesus ascended into heaven on a cloud[127] and as tongues of fire came down on His disciples at Pentecost.[128]

---

[124] Philippians 2:6-8.
[125] Acts 2:33.
[126] Luke 24:1-12.
[127] Acts 1:9-11.
[128] Acts 2:1-3.

They did not take Jesus for granted then; they did not wonder what to do about the glory. They did not keep silent.[129]

Nor shall we.

৯৽৶

---

[129] Acts 2:4.

## Luke 10:25-37 RSV

[25] *And behold, a lawyer stood up to put [Jesus] to the test, saying, "Teacher, what shall I do to inherit eternal life?"*

[26] *He said to him, "What is written in the law? How do you read?"*

[27] *And he answered, "You shall love the Lord your God with all your heart, and with all your soul, and with all your strength, and with all our mind; and your neighbor as yourself."*

[28] *And he said to him, "You have answered right; do this, and you will live."*

[29] *But he, desiring to justify himself, said to Jesus, "And who is my neighbor?"*

[30] *Jesus replied, "A man was going down from Jerusalem to Jericho, and he fell among robbers, who stripped him and beat him, and departed, leaving him half dead.* [31] *Now by chance a priest was going down that road; and when he saw him he passed by on the other side.* [32] *So likewise a Levite, when he came to the place and saw him, passed by on the other side.* [33] *But a Samaritan, as he journeyed, came to where he was; and when he saw him, he had compassion,* [34] *and went to him and bound up his wounds, pouring on oil and wine; then he set him on his own beast and brought him to an inn, and took care of him.* [35] *And the next day he took out two denarii and gave them to the innkeeper, saying, 'Take care of him; and whatever more you spend, I will repay you when I come back.'* [36] *Which of these three, do you think, proved neighbor to the man who fell among the robbers?"*

[37] *He said, "The one who showed mercy on him."*

*And Jesus said to him, "Go and do likewise."*

# 14.

# What to Do—Who to Be

## Luke 10:25-37 RSV

We're in luck today. Today, we look at the Good Samaritan. The Parable of the Good Samaritan is a great story—one of the best Jesus ever told. Of course, the story didn't just pop up out of nowhere. Jesus didn't just give a whistle one day and say, "Hey, everybody, listen to this neat story I just thought up." Jesus told this story to answer a question—or rather, to ask a question of His own on His way to answering another one.

The story of the Good Samaritan is always worth repeating. But this time, listen very carefully, as though you're hearing it for the first time. You need to hear the story in its context to appreciate its purpose.

For instance, notice what's going on here. A lawyer stands up to ask Jesus a question. The lawyer, in this case, is really a kind of Bible scholar, an expert on the Law of Moses found in the first five books of our Bibles.

His job is to know and explain—*and* enforce—all the rules God gave Moses "way back when" for the children of Israel. Moses is long gone now, but the rules are still there, and the lawyers just keep on memorizing and explaining and enforcing them. And there seems to be some confusion about what Jesus thinks about this process, so this particular lawyer has decided to check Him out.

Luke says the fellow stands up (a sign of respect) and calls Jesus, "Teacher" (also a sign of respect). But what the lawyer really means to do behind the façade of respect is to trip Jesus up with some tricky question. No matter how Jesus answers, the lawyer means to make Him look bad. It's kind of like what present-day reporters do at some of these political press conferences. But it won't be long before this fellow will wish he had kept his seat firmly planted on the ground and his words securely locked in his mouth—'cause Jesus ain't like no politician he ever saw!

If you look carefully, you will see that there are two rounds of questions and answers in what Luke records. In each round, the lawyer asks Jesus a question and Jesus responds with a question of His own. The lawyer, finding the tables turned by the question of Jesus, and himself (the lawyer) on the spot, reluctantly answers the question Jesus has put to him. And based on the lawyer's answer, Jesus responds to the original question.

The lawyer initiates the first round trying to score a moral and intellectual victory over Jesus. He initiates the second round hoping merely to avoid a humiliating defeat.

Poor lawyer! He doesn't stand a chance.

And where does the famous parable fit in?

It's just an illustration that sets up the question Jesus puts to the lawyer in "the second round." We'll get there in a minute.

క్తింగ

Let's look first at the lawyer's "trick" question: "What should I do to inherit eternal life?"

The subject—eternal life—is certainly worth discussing. Jesus talks about it a lot—and He's not the only one. We probably ought to talk about it more ourselves—more than we do.

It was widely understood that eternal life was something you inherited, but the lawyer wants to know what he can "do" to make sure that he will inherit it. But really, about the only thing you can "do" to inherit something is to arrange it so that you are born the child of a parent who is going to bequeath that something to his or her heirs as an inheritance.

The lawyer asks Jesus, *"What shall I do…,"* as though there is some precise minimum that will get you into heaven with the least amount of wasted effort: "What, when I've done it, will cause me to inherit eternal life?"

Of course, the lawyer doesn't think Jesus knows what that minimum effort is. But Jesus, to the surprise of the lawyer, plays along, and, to his greater surprise, turns the tables on him: "So what do you think it will take to inherit eternal life? What is the official answer?"

All eyes in the group swivel around from Jesus to the lawyer. The lawyer swallows, and answers with a combination of Old Testament commandments calling for unconditional love of God[130] and neighbor.[131] It appears to have been a popular answer to the question among the authorities discussing it. Jesus Himself offers just such an answer in other Gospels[132] when asked about "the greatest commandment"—which sounds like the same question, but isn't. The lawyer may, in fact, be quoting the very words of Jesus back to Him.

Whatever the case, when the lawyer finishes what he has to say, Jesus says, "Yea, that'll do. Do that."

But He doesn't say that the lawyer will *"inherit eternal life"* for doing it. Jesus says, "Love God and your neighbor (in a constant and complete way) and you will 'come alive.'"

Jesus isn't *dis*-interested in eternity; He just knows that it can't be separated from the life we live in the present. And the lawyer knows that even though Jesus has readily agreed with his answer, there is something wrong with it, nonetheless.

---

[130] Deuteronomy 6:5.

[131] Leviticus 19:18.

[132] Matthew 22:34-40.

Our problem is not that we don't *know* what to *do* to inherit eternal life. The problem is that we *know* that what we *do doesn't* get the job done, and what *would* get the job done, we are not *able* or *willing* (if we're honest with ourselves) to do.

Paul said in Romans, *"I can will what is right, but I cannot do it. For I do not do the good I want, but the evil I do not want is what I do."*[133] The problem ain't knowing what to do; the problem is doing what you know!

∂∾⊰

Well, things aren't going the way the lawyer thought they would when he decided to bushwhack Jesus, but he can't just let it go and cut his losses.

So: Round Two.

"If loving God and my neighbor is the answer, who is my neighbor?"

The legalistic mind gets the requirement—and just naturally starts trying to whittle it down a little—shaving off the hard edges and molding it into a form that feels more manageable. Like the lawyer, we want God to "grade on the curve"—and then, "round up!"

"How small can I draw the circle around me and still have all the people who qualify as neighbors fit inside of it?"

And a question like *that* calls for a story that goes like *this*: "*A man was going down from Jerusalem to Jericho,*" says Jesus. And this man is going to have a worse time of it even than the lawyer is having with Jesus.

The way from Jerusalem to Jericho is 17 miles of desert road, and a big band of bloodthirsty bandits own it.[134] The bandits attack

---

[133] Romans 7:18-19, RSV.

[134] The historical, cultural details that follow are drawn from Kenneth E. Bailey's treatment of the parable in *Poet & Peasant and Through Peasant Eyes: A Literary-Cultural Approach to the Parables of Jesus*, Grand Rapids, MI: William B. Eerdmans Publishing Company, 1983, (Book II) pp. 33-56.

the man, take his money and strip him bare. They beat him senseless and leave him for dead. All in all, not very neighborly of them.

The man's clothes or his accent could have told you a lot about who he was. But they left him nothing your eyes or ears could recognize.

Is he your neighbor? Who knows?

A priest doesn't know. There's one riding along because priests are important men in a religious country and important people ride. He's heading home from his priestly service in the Jerusalem Temple, ritually pure and, therefore, fully qualified to disperse the perks of his sacred service to family and friends waiting at the other end of his "sacred" journey.

The rules say getting too close to a dead body will defile a priest[135] and send him back to the Temple—to pay in time and expense and public disgrace—while another priest *re*-purifies him. The rules say touching a "foreigner" will defile a priest with the same results.

Is this a "foreigner"?

The priest can't tell.

Is the poor fellow dead?

Could be. And why take the chance?

Is he a "neighbor"?

Who knows?

The rules say, "Get on down the road!"

And the priest obeys the rules.

৯৽৽৸

But, *my!*—it's a busy road. A Levite follows the priest. He's kind of like the Chaplains' Assistants in the military[136]—or maybe the deacon in a civilian church. The Levite helps the priest in the

---

[135] Leviticus 21:1-2; Numbers 19:11.
[136] In the Navy, Marine Corps and Coast Guard, these enlisted men and women are known as Religious Program Specialists.

Temple and knows the priest is somewhere up ahead. Then the Levite sees this bloody, naked body on the side of the road. But he sees no priest.

This is a lesson in leadership, and though the rules aren't as strict on the religious workers like the Levite as they are on the priest, it would be "rude" for the Levite to outshine his "spiritual betters" in compassion or kindness.

Is this poor wretch a "neighbor"?

The priest apparently didn't think so, and there's nothing to suggest to the Levite that the priest was wrong. So the Levite follows the priest, in more ways than one.

୬∽୶

And who's next?

In a normal story, it should by rights be the Jewish layman who attended the Temple service led by the priest who was supported by the Levite. This Jewish "everyman" is the logical "next" on the scene. And he will be a popular hero for the story being told to a group of everyday Jews, because we like our heroes to look like us.

But Jesus brings somebody else down the Jericho Road. It's the last man on earth the lawyer or anybody else in the audience would have expected—or wanted—to turn up at this point in the story.

*"A Samaritan, as he journeyed, came to where he was...."*

Now *here's* a "foreigner"—and more likely to end up a dead man at the hands of Jewish bandits than anybody else on that road. Many listening to the story would have volunteered to kill him themselves.

What's the big deal about a Samaritan?

Well, substitute "Israeli," if you're Palestinian—or "Muslim fundamentalist" if you lost someone on September 11th. If you are pro-life, make him an abortionist. Make him a Klansman if you're black. Imagine the group of human beings you hate the most, and they are your "Samaritans."

And Jesus has just put one of them on a burrow and sent him down the road to the place where the stranger lies, badly hurt, helpless and alone. But stand by, Jesus is about to make your Samaritan the only good guy in your world.

Jesus can do this because He knows that "neighbor" is not about *who* one *is*, but about *what* one *does*. The Samaritan doesn't know who this poor soul lying alongside the road ahead of him is. Friend or foe, he cannot know. Stripped of everything, the unknown man is now known for who he is: He is simply a human being in need.

The bandits and the priest and the Levite decided that he was not their neighbor and treated him, each in their turn, accordingly. The Samaritan saw this man for who he was and had a different reaction: *"He had compassion on him."*

The Samaritan decided, *"I* am *his* neighbor," and made up for all the others. He administered the first aid the Levite could have provided but didn't. The Samaritan placed the bloody fellow on his own burrow as the priest could have done, and led the man, as a servant would, to safety. The Samaritan took his own money to pay for the stranger's needs, just as the bandits had taken the unconscious man's money when they left him in need. The Samaritan risked so much more than anyone else, not because he knew who the stranger was, but because he knew who *he* was.

☙❧

The lawyer knows, too, because the point of the story is the question Jesus now puts to him: "Who is the neighbor in this story?"

And though he cannot bring himself to even speak the hated name, the lawyer cannot avoid the answer: "The neighbor is *'the one who showed mercy.'"* A Jewish scholar is then told: "Go and follow the example of a Samaritan businessman. You have to do what he did if you want to live."

Jesus tells the lawyer: "Go and do…" But He really means: "Go and *be*…," because you cannot do what the Good Samaritan does until you feel the gut-filling compassion for people the Samaritan felt for that poor stranger. You'll have to have a heart and spirit like the Samaritan, of all people.

And how likely is that?

Well, maybe if you've had a Good Samaritan have compassion for you and pick you up and bind your wounds and ease your pain and meet your needs and give you back your life when it wasn't worth calling a life—then what the Good Samaritan did to you might change you into a Good Samaritan, too—or something a lot more like one than what you were before He came along—or would ever be, if He had never come your way at all.

&#8766;

The Good Samaritan isn't a real person, of course. He's a fictional character in a story. Jesus just made him up to make a point. The Good Samaritan isn't a real person…

…or is He?

The enemies of Jesus accuse Him of being a Samaritan and demon-possessed.[137] He rejects the demon possession part, but lets the Samaritan remark go by without a word. They mean it as a vicious insult, but Jesus doesn't take it too hard. And if anyone could fill that particular Samaritan's "shoes," it's Jesus.

Jesus doesn't care who you are or how great your need. He doesn't care what other people—even important people—think about you or have done to you. He doesn't care what it has and will cost Him to take care of you—to save your life and make you well and get you home. He doesn't care about any of that because He cares so much about *you.*

What can you *do* to inherit eternal life?

---

[137] John 8:48.

Nothing, really.

But you can let Jesus be the Neighbor Who shows you divine mercy so that you can come alive and be a neighbor like Him to all you encounter in need.

Do this and you will live.

శ్రీ

## Luke 10:25-37 RSV

<sup>25</sup> *And behold, a lawyer stood up to put [Jesus] to the test, saying, "Teacher, what shall I do to inherit eternal life?"*

<sup>26</sup> *He said to him, "What is written in the law? How do you read?"*

<sup>27</sup> *And he answered, "You shall love the Lord your God with all your heart, and with all your soul, and with all your strength, and with all our mind; and your neighbor as yourself."*

<sup>28</sup> *And he said to him, "You have answered right; do this, and you will live."*

<sup>29</sup> *But he, desiring to justify himself, said to Jesus, "And who is my neighbor?"*

<sup>30</sup> *Jesus replied, "A man was going down from Jerusalem to Jericho, and he fell among robbers, who stripped him and beat him, and departed, leaving him half dead.* <sup>31</sup> *Now by chance a priest was going down that road; and when he saw him he passed by on the other side.* <sup>32</sup> *So likewise a Levite, when he came to the place and saw him, passed by on the other side.* <sup>33</sup> *But a Samaritan, as he journeyed, came to where he was; and when he saw him, he had compassion,* <sup>34</sup> *and went to him and bound up his wounds, pouring on oil and wine; then he set him on his own beast and brought him to an inn, and took care of him.* <sup>35</sup> *And the next day he took out two denarii and gave them to the innkeeper, saying, 'Take care of him; and whatever more you spend, I will repay you when I come back.'* <sup>36</sup> *Which of these three, do you think, proved neighbor to the man who fell among the robbers?"*

<sup>37</sup> *He said, "The one who showed mercy on him."*

*And Jesus said to him, "Go and do likewise."*

જ⚬ક

# 15.

# From Jerusalem to Jericho

## Luke 10:25-37 RSV

There is a road that runs from Jerusalem down to Jericho. It's an old road—centuries old—not the one that cars travel today. The old road from Jerusalem to Jericho is a steep and lonely road, beginning in the Mediterranean lushness of Jerusalem atop Mount Zion and dropping over half a mile in altitude into dry and rocky desert as it winds its way down to Jericho, 17 miles away.[138]

A man could walk down that road from Jerusalem to Jericho in six or seven hours. Going up the other way would take several hours more. Many people who traveled that road did not make it to their destination; they fell victim to robbers—they were attacked along the way. It was a dangerous road, this road from Jerusalem to Jericho.

Jesus knew this road. He had walked it, up and down, and He would do so again, at least once. And one day, He made it the setting for a story about the journey we are all taking together. One day, He put *you* on that road from Jerusalem down to Jericho.

---

[138] John Wilkinson, "The Way from Jerusalem to Jericho," *The Biblical Archaeologist*, Vol. 38, No. 1 (March., 1975), pp. 10-24.

You know the story: Someone is going down this road and is jumped by a bunch of thugs who take everything worth taking and beat the person almost to death. Then two people—religious people—come along, one after the other, and do nothing. They just keep on going, down the road.

Then somebody else comes along—somebody you wouldn't expect to be on that road—somebody you don't even like and certainly don't trust. And yet that's the person who turns out to be kind and compassionate, attentive and generous—to be the hero—the life saver.

And if you are not disturbed by the story, you haven't been listening. Oh, it's a wonderful thing that the victim in the story is saved—that a hero appears. And that unlikely hero has been raised up and immortalized across the centuries as a noble example for everyone to emulate.

But the one who turns out to be the hero is "the enemy"—someone instinctively hated and vilified—someone you would think more likely to finish a helpless victim off than furnish medicine and cover the cost of recuperation.

❧

And there's the problem with the parable: Since the hero you are expecting to identify with turns out to be your enemy, you're left with the not-so-noble priest and Levite as your role model options. They are religious, like you. They are going home after their participation in the worship of their God, as you will do at the end of this service. But you don't want to be like the priest and the Levite. You certainly don't want to be *seen* to look like them.

And yet, you know how they feel. You know the calculations they are making between common decency and common sense, and why they are coming out on the side of self-preservation rather than risking themselves in response to the need of this poor stranger on the road. You know why they pass by on the other side and proceed on down the road. And you instinctively defend them.

But you are not happy with the choice they—and you—have had to confront—or the course of action they have taken.

It's a disturbing story.

It's a dangerous road.

❧

You go down the road, hoping to get to your destination without incident. You hope everything will go all right, but you know the longer you go, the rougher the road will become. The longer you go down this road, the more good things you will leave behind.

You know there are hazards along the way—there are hidden dangers, including hostile people "who will hurt you and desert you and take your soul if you let them,"[139] to quote a song from my youth. And many who would not go out of their way to hurt you, will also not go out of their way to help you when you need it.

And what is worse—what is more disturbing even than what you are likely to suffer on the road from the hardship of the road itself and the hostility or neglect of other people—is the pattern of failures in your own performance as a person of faith. You cannot walk this road in peace because your best intentions and worst fears are always at war within you.

How many times have you wanted to help someone and found yourself saying, "I can't do that"?

If you're religious—if you take the moral teaching of Jesus seriously—even a little bit—you won't get far down this road without picking up a heavy load of guilt and shame to weigh you down and attack you spiritually, just like those thugs attacked their victim physically.

Jesus walked this road. So did Paul. Paul could have been right here on this road when he wrote: *"I do not do what I want, but I do the very thing I hate.... I can will what is right, but I cannot do it.... I do not do*

---

[139] Carole King, "You Need a Friend," 1971.

*the good I want, but the evil I do not want is what I do.... Wretched man that I am! Who will deliver me from this body of death?"*[140]

If the world doesn't beat you up, your conscience will. And if it doesn't, it should. You see a victim of the cunning and cruelty of this world, and you stop—or you don't. And if you do stop to help this time, before long, there's another victim and another, all needing help. And if your compassion ever overruled your caution, your reservoir of concern will run out long before the need will.

And you end up passing so many by that the moral conflict inside leaves you a victim, too—it strips you of the most valuable thing you have: your godly heart.

And who will stop and help *you*?

৵৽

*"But a Samaritan, as he journeyed, came to where he was; and when he saw him, he had compassion, and went to him and bound up his wounds, pouring on oil and wine; then he set him on his own beast and brought him to an inn, and took care of him."*

৵৽

Strange things happen on this road. Unexpected people stop and help you. Compassion and healing come from the hand you would be inclined to slap away, if you could. But when you no longer have it in you to choose your own hero—your own savior— the One God sends, comes.

The Samaritan should not have been on that road. It was not his road. It was more dangerous for him to be there than for the poor victim who had no consciousness of his help. The Samaritan did not have to help. This was not his friend or family. The religious people, as he knew, had not helped.

But the Samaritan—the despised and rejected—and Good— Samaritan—was there on that road, going down from Jerusalem to

---

[140] Romans 7:15, 19, 24, RSV.

Jericho. And he was the person who saw the need and stopped and bound up the wounds and brought one helpless stranger to a place of safety to recover from what had happened on the road—the road from Jerusalem down to Jericho.

Jesus knows this road. He made it the setting for a story about the journey we are all taking together. Jesus walked this road, up and down, because it is both the road from Jerusalem down to Jericho and the road from Jericho up to Jerusalem. And the last time Jesus will walk it, He will be walking the harder way. He will be going up to Jerusalem—going up the road to the place where violent men will strip Him and beat Him and leave Him—dead.

Jesus will go up that road to become the Victim Who is despised and rejected—Who is hated by His own people as passionately as they hate their Samaritan neighbors.

A Samaritan, traveling down the road from Jerusalem to Jericho, saw a stranger in need and had compassion on him and did what he could to save him. And like that Samaritan, Jesus traveled up that same road to Jerusalem where He saw an estranged humanity and had compassion upon every dying one and did what only He could do to save us all.

Though others have passed you by in your need—though you have passed others by in their need—Jesus has not passed you by. He has compassion on your suffering—He has mercy and grace for your guilt—and He comes to you, to bind up your wounds and take you where you can be cared for and cured of the injuries you have sustained, whether from the journey itself or the hostility of others, or the injuries you have inflicted upon yourself—on that road we all are traveling together.

The Samaritan took the poor stranger he had rescued to a place where he could be cared for, and he told the people there, *"Take care of him; and...I will repay you when I come back."*

Jesus has rescued all of you and taken you to a place where you can be cared for as you recover from the wounds He has bound up. Jesus is bringing more poor, rescued souls all the time. What is it He says? "Take care of them and I will repay you when I come back."

But Jesus says something else. He points to that unexpected and unsettling Samaritan and says, *"Go and do likewise."*

It's good here where He put us to get us cared for, and it's good to care for others while we're here, but that old road is still out there and it's still our road and theirs—a road with hazards we and they succumb to, and so therefore a road in need of Samaritans—good Samaritans—Samaritans like Jesus and those He has cared for and commissioned to serve Him—and with Him—on that road.

Who is the neighbor?

A Samaritan.

A Savior.

And you?

৯৩

# 16.

# The Problem with Having Too Much

## Luke 12:13-21 ESV

*[13] Someone in the crowd said to [Jesus], "Teacher, tell my brother to divide the inheritance with me." [14] But he said to him, "Man, who made me a judge or arbitrator over you?" [15] And he said to them, "Take care, and be on your guard against all covetousness, for one's life does not consist in the abundance of his possessions." [16] And he told them a parable, saying, "The land of a rich man produced plentifully, [17] and he thought to himself, 'What shall I do, for I have nowhere to store my crops?' [18] And he said, 'I will do this: I will tear down my barns and build larger ones, and there I will store all my grain and my goods. [19] And I will say to my soul, "Soul, you have ample goods laid up for many years; relax, eat, drink, be merry."' [20] But God said to him, 'Fool! This night your soul is required of you, and the things you have prepared, whose will they be?' [21] So is the one who lays up treasure for himself and is not rich toward God."*

❧❧

It appears from the story we heard today that Jesus has no sympathy for "the greedy poor" and no respect for "the greedy rich." Jesus rebuffs the man who wants Jesus to take property from his brother and give it to him. And in refusing to redistribute the wealth from a "have" to a "have not," Jesus tells a story condemning another "have" who will not redistribute his own wealth. Is it any wonder that Jesus mystified people?

And between His rejection of the demand that He enforce economic justice and His telling of the parable, Jesus offered a warning to everyone in his audience—and to everyone in this chapel: "Be on your guard against all kinds of greed, because your life does not consist in how much you have."

&#8766;

You see, the issue is not wealth.

It's greed.

Greed comes in many forms—and none of them are good.[141] Greed is a natural human instinct—a sinful instinct. We don't need to be taught greed; we're born with it. And all too often, we nurture it through life.

You don't have to have anything to be greedy. Greed isn't so much about having as it is about wanting. It's as much about wanting things you don't have as it is about wanting more of what you do have. It's about wanting to keep what you have—for yourself.

It's actually possible to have quite a lot and not be greedy. The man in the parable is not condemned because he is wealthy. He is condemned because of what he thinks about his wealth, and what he decides to do with it as a result. He is already rich when the story starts. Jesus does not say he did anything wrong in getting rich or in increasing his wealth. Christian moral values have enabled many of us to prosper in life.

&#8766;

But the rich man thinks *he* is responsible for his prosperity; Jesus says, *"the land...produced abundantly."* The rich man thinks

---

[141] Contrary to the now famous assertion of Michael Douglas' character, Gordon Gekko, in the movie *Wall Street*, 1987.

he has the right and the authority to decide what to do with the surplus.

He sees it as *his* crop. And so he will have *his* barns torn down and store *his* grain and *his* goods in the bigger barns *he* will have built. He even talks about *his* soul and *his* future—as if they are his possessions as well.

The poor rich man has been blessed with abundance and he thinks that it is all his doing—and that the appropriate thing to do is to hold on to it all and expend it for his own personal pleasure.

So he builds his bigger barns. He moves his surplus there. And he is ready to enjoy the rest of his life—except that it turns out his soul was on loan from God, and his life was on loan from God, and everything he possessed was on loan from God.

And when God called in the loan on his life, he lost everything he thought he possessed at the same time.

Everything the wealthy man thought was his—wasn't. All that he had, it turns out, was God's alone,[142] a temporary gift—to an otherwise poor man—from an infinitely generous God.

And, in fact, even with all that God gave him, he remained a poor man, because he misused what God gave him. He misused it because he misunderstood its purpose.

God gives wealth for two reasons, according to the New Testament. One is so that you will not be a burden to others,[143] and the second is so that you will be able to help those in need.[144] The man in the parable had too much for himself—for his own needs. But what was too much for him, was just enough to help others in need. But he did not help others with the surplus.

❧

---

[142] See the hymn, "We Give Thee But Thine Own," by William Walsham How, 1868.
[143] 2 Thessalonians 2:7-12.
[144] Ephesians 4:28.

And what is worse, as far as Jesus is concerned, the man did not help himself. The bigger barns he built in his greed became his prison where the things he possessed held him captive, alone and isolated from the God Who gave him both his surplus and his neighbors—neighbors who needed his surplus far more than he did. By defining his life in terms of his possessions, he cut the cord of living relationship with God and his community.

That's the problem with having too much. If you have too much, you've been storing up treasures for yourself.

Accumulating treasure by moral means is all right with God—all we have is a gift on loan from God. But to hoard the excess is to become poor toward the God Who gives all—and takes it all away.[145]

Jesus was unwilling to take property from a man and give it to the brother who wanted it. Jesus was more concerned about the spirit of greed He heard in the voice of the one who called out to Him.

But suppose the one in possession of the land had cared enough about his brother's need—and his God's intention—that he had chosen to provide for his brother from the surplus of his abundance. Both men might have become rich in the only way that truly matters: rich toward God.

&ominus;

---

[145] Job 1:21.

# 17.

# Hypocrite or Healed?

## Luke 13:10-17 ESV

*[10] Now [Jesus] was teaching in one of the synagogues on the Sabbath.
[11] And behold, there was a woman who had had a disabling spirit for eighteen
years. She was bent over and could not fully straighten herself. [12] When Jesus
saw her, he called her over and said to her, "Woman, you are freed from your
disability." [13] And he laid his hands on her, and immediately she was made
straight, and she glorified God. [14] But the ruler of the synagogue, indignant
because Jesus had healed on the Sabbath, said to the people, "There are six
days in which work ought to be done. Come on those days and be healed, and
not on the Sabbath day." [15] Then the Lord answered him, "You hypocrites!
Does not each of you on the Sabbath untie his ox or his donkey from the
manger and lead it away to water it? [16] And ought not this woman, a daughter
of Abraham whom Satan bound for eighteen years, be loosed from this bond
on the Sabbath day?" [17] As he said these things, all his adversaries were put
to shame, and all the people rejoiced at all the glorious things that were done by
him.*

❧

    The Gospel reading today is one of those passages that, for us,
is like looking through a very foggy window—or as Paul would say,

*"a glass darkly."*[146] You probably get the general shape of things, but a lot of the detail—and, therefore, the meaning—has been obscured by the significant differences in culture, language and perspective that have built up over the centuries. Let's clean the window and get a better look.

One Saturday, Jesus turns up at a men's Bible study held every week at the Jewish community center in an unnamed Galilean village. Many things take place in this community center, or synagogue, but on their Sabbath, or holy day, which is Saturday, the men of the village gather to read and discuss the Jewish Torah, their scripture. This is what passes for a worship service for those who do not live close enough to go to the Temple in Jerusalem.

It's a men's study. Women and children may observe from a distance, but they are not allowed to participate.

Of course, when a controversial and fascinating rabbi like Jesus shows up, attendance goes up. Everybody wants to have a look at Jesus. But what many don't realize is that Jesus looks back at them—and sees a lot more than they do.

⤝⤜

Working His way through the crowd to the synagogue, for instance, Jesus sees a woman doubled over. Everybody else sees her all the time and so they don't "see" her at all anymore. But Jesus does.

He not only sees her, He calls attention to her. That, by itself, is bordering on the socially inappropriate. He calls her into the center of their gathering—which means He speaks to her in public, which the custom says a man should not do.

And what He says to her is even more astonishing. What He says to her only God had the right to say: *"Woman, you are freed from your infirmity."*

---

[146] 1 Corinthians 13:12, KJV.

And just when you think Jesus can't violate any more of the social and religious proprieties, He touches the woman.

Godly men do not touch women they are not related to—ever, for any reason! They don't even touch their wives in public. But Jesus put His hands on this woman He has never seen before.

The men in the synagogue do not see the woman, but they certainly see what Jesus does to her when *He* sees her. They hear what He says. You can describe their reaction in one word: "indignant."

"Somebody ought to say something!"

And the leader of the Bible study does. But he doesn't say it to Jesus; he says it to the crowd watching Jesus. "You all ignore this and go home. There's a time and place for everything, and this isn't it!"

❧

Isn't it sad when people spend their time studying God's Word and don't learn anything?

Jesus saw the woman and what she needed and gave it to her. He now sees what the members of this men's group need, and He gives it to them—*in spades*!

"You hypocrites! You treat your animals better than your brothers and sisters! The time and place for doing the work of God is whenever and wherever you see work that needs to be done. And you ought to be looking all the time."

The woman outside the synagogue had been in bondage to a bent-over body for 18 years and Jesus straightened out that problem for her. He gave her a normal life again.

But how many in the village were "bent over" spiritually—and had been for far longer? Just as His gentle touch was intended to straighten up the woman's back, so His firm hand with the hypocrites of the village was intended to straighten out their twisted souls.

When you see clearly what's going on, you'll understand Jesus better.

And when you see what Jesus does—when you hear what He says—the question then becomes: Are you delighted or humiliated?

And even that doesn't really matter, except as it determines your response to Him.

Will you remain crippled by a disabling spirit—or straightened out by the divine Christ?

❧

## Isaiah 25:6-9 ESV

$^6$ On this mountain
the LORD of hosts will make for all peoples
    a feast of rich food,
    a feast of well-aged wine,
    of rich food full of marrow,
    of aged wine well refined.
$^7$ And he will swallow up on this mountain
    the covering that is cast over all peoples,
    the veil that is spread over all nations.
$^8$ He will swallow up death forever;
    and the Lord GOD will wipe away
        tears from all faces,
    and the reproach of his people
    he will take away from all the earth,
        for the LORD has spoken.
$^9$ It will be said on that day,
"Behold, this is our God;
    we have waited for him,
        that he might save us.
This is the LORD;
    we have waited for him;
        let us be glad and rejoice
        in his salvation."

&#10086;&#10087;

## Luke 14:1, 12-24 ESV

$^1$ *One Sabbath, when [Jesus] went to dine at the house of a ruler of the Pharisees, they were watching him carefully.*

$^{12}$ *He said also to the man who had invited him, "When you give a dinner or a banquet, do not invite your friends or your brothers or your relatives or rich neighbors, lest they also invite you in return and you be repaid. $^{13}$ But when you give a feast, invite the poor, the crippled, the lame, the blind, $^{14}$ and you will be blessed, because they cannot repay you. For you will be repaid at the resurrection of the just."*

$^{15}$ *When one of those who reclined at table with him heard these things, he said to him, "Blessed is everyone who will eat bread in the kingdom of God!" $^{16}$ But he said to him, "A man once gave a great banquet and invited many. $^{17}$ And at the time for the banquet he sent his servant to say to those who had been invited, 'Come, for everything is now ready.' $^{18}$ But they all alike began to make excuses. The first said to him, 'I have bought a field, and I must go out and see it. Please have me excused.' $^{19}$ And another said, 'I have bought five yoke of oxen, and I go to examine them. Please have me excused.' $^{20}$ And another said, 'I have married a wife, and therefore I cannot come.' $^{21}$ So the servant came and reported these things to his master. Then the master of the house became angry and said to his servant, 'Go out quickly to the streets and lanes of the city, and bring in the poor and crippled and blind and lame.' $^{22}$ And the servant said, 'Sir, what you commanded has been done, and still there is room.' $^{23}$ And the master said to the servant, 'Go out to the highways and hedges and compel people to come in, that my house may be filled. $^{24}$ For I tell you, none of those men who were invited shall taste my banquet.'"*

৯~৯

# 18.

# Are You Going to the Party?

## Isaiah 25:6-9; Luke 14:1, 12-24 ESV

Jesus is attending another one of those dinner parties that isn't likely to end well. He's been invited to a formal banquet on a Sabbath by a Pharisee who's also brought in a bunch of Bible lawyers to mark every word Jesus says and watch His every move so they can pounce on Him for anything outside their definition of "acceptable."

So Jesus heals a man—on the Sabbath—which is certainly frowned on in their religious circles. Jesus gives His host some unsolicited advice about who to invite to his parties in the future, and His fellow guests get some pointed suggestions about how to behave better at the present party.

And when somebody tries to change the subject and diffuse the tension Jesus has created, Jesus just piles more on by telling what, to their ears, is a bizarre and ultimately stinging story about who will end up going to the greatest party of all.[147]

---

[147] Again, the historical and cultural details of the setting and the story are drawn from Kenneth E. Bailey's parable studies in *Poet & Peasant and Through Peasant Eyes: A Literary-Cultural Approach to the Parables of Jesus*, Grand Rapids, MI: William B. Eerdmans Publishing Company, 1983, (Book II) pp. 88-113.

It's another one of those "different culture—different meaning—different impact" stories.

დ⊷ჿ

Jesus says, *"A certain man was preparing a great banquet and invited many guests. At the time of the banquet, he sent his servant to tell those who had been invited, 'Come, for everything is now ready.'"*

Here's how it worked: If you wanted to throw a party, you sent a servant to recite your invitation, word for word from memory, to every person you were inviting. The invitation was brief—to the point—and included time, date, place and purpose of the party. When you heard the invitation, you told the servant if you were able to attend, and the servant would relay your acceptance to the host, who would then determine what kind of animals—and how many—to kill and cook, based on the number of guests who agreed to come.

დ⊷ჿ

Many of the finest folks were invited by this great man. Many of them accepted his generous invitation. It would be a great banquet—a real party! Every one of the guests knew that the servant would come back when the food was ready to say just what Jesus says he would say: *"Come, for everything is now ready."*

So far, so good.

But when the servant came—when the invited guests were told that everything is ready for the party they said they would come to, *"they all,"* according to Jesus, *"began to make excuses."* And listen to these excuses!

*"I have [just] bought a field, and I must go and see it."*

You've already bought it and *now* you're going to go look at it?

Nobody buys agricultural property in Palestine without knowing every inch of it before the bargaining begins.

And besides, banquets begin at sundown. How much detail of a field are you going to see in the dark? And won't the field be there in the morning? Why *must* you see it tonight? And what were you doing *this* morning about seeing the field when you knew you had agreed to go to a banquet tonight?

This isn't an excuse; this is an intentional and very public insult to the host of the banquet.

But the servant hears what the man has to say—and moves on to the next guest.

*"I have just bought five yoke of oxen, and I'm on my way to try them out."*

You're going to find out if they're any good *after* you've already paid for them?

That's not how it's done in Palestine. You take oxen—all of them—for a "test plow" *before* you start the dickering.

It would be like somebody today buying a fleet of trucks for his company and not knowing what make or model they are, what the gas mileage is or the payload capacity, or their maintenance history. Oh, and do you really think you're going to learn anything about these animals by plowing with them—five pairs of them— in the dark?

Doesn't matter. He's on his way already, and good thing the servant found him in time to find out that he isn't coming to the party he agreed to attend.

A valid excuse?

Not hardly!

But at least these two had the pretense of etiquette to cover themselves by saying, *"Please, excuse me."*

With the third invited guest, it gets worse.

❧

In our day and age, you can hardly go anywhere without stumbling across people who will gladly give you far more information about their love life than you ever wanted to hear.

But that's not the way it was—or is—in the Middle Eastern world. A man doesn't talk openly about, or even allude to, the women in his family—and especially not his relationship with his wife. But the third excuse?

*"I married a wife—and I can't come."*

Well, at least he didn't subject the servant to hearing what he was going to do with this wife that would prevent his keeping his promise to come to the party—what couldn't be put off for a few hours while he fulfilled his obligation of honor to the host who had gone out of his way to honor this guest. And this third guest doesn't even pretend to be polite while snubbing the host at the last minute: "I'm not coming."

What's up with these guys?!

They've been invited to a great party by someone who apparently thinks of them as treasured friends—by someone who has gone to great expense and bother to treat them like royalty. Why would they spit in his face this way?

And you can be sure that when his servant tells him what they've said, the host will understand perfectly that they have intentionally and cynically insulted him. And he will feel what you would expect him to feel: fierce anger.

❧

But if what the guests have done is stunning, so is what the host does in response. Yes, he's angry about what they've done, but he doesn't call off the banquet. He can't let his great sacrifice go to waste. There *is* going to be a party—for somebody.

And so this remarkable, generous host sends the servant out again to invite the kind of folks nobody thought would ever have a chance to go to a great party. *They* don't even think they're the kind of folks who would be invited to this kind of a party, and so the servant has to go to some trouble to convince them that they really are invited.

But no matter. As far as the host is concerned, there *will* be a great banquet and the place *will* be filled—whatever it takes to get people to come in. The place will be filled for this great banquet because the servant, as directed, has invited—everybody.

So go figure: All those people who were invited and had a wonderful place all ready for them at the party blew it all off and won't be there when they could have been—and tons of people who had no reason to ever expect or even hope to get into a party like this one are going to be having the time of their lives after all, just because they accepted an unexpected and unbelievable invitation to come. An amazing parable, as all the stories of Jesus are.

സ്

But don't assume He's just talking to those high and mighty Pharisees who invited Him to dinner to do a number on Him. How many of our friends and neighbors—how many of us—have heard the sacred Servant of our heavenly banquet Host offer that heartfelt invitation to join in the great party He has put together for us, and yet decided, inexplicably, that something absolutely absurd was more important than being a part of the greatest party ever?

How many people today are walking away from the faith they were raised with? How many have convinced themselves that there will be no party, or that the invitation is a fake?

On September 15th, we will take part in "National Back to Church Sunday" as the beginning for a month-long emphasis renewing the invitation to that great, God-sponsored banquet that Isaiah foretold and Jesus brought about. Of course, every Sunday is "Back to Church Sunday" for all who need to receive the invitation they once rejected.

Every Sunday is "accept-God's-invitation-in-Christ-to-come-to-the-great-banquet-in-heaven Sunday."

Being here indicates a desire to do just that. Gathering around these communion tables is a way of previewing the banquet that awaits you.

And then that time comes—as it did for one of our beloved sisters this week—when God's Messenger appears to you and tells you, "All is now ready for you." And the eternal celebration begins in earnest for each one who has accepted God's glorious invitation.

"The [banquet] table of the Lord is set before you [in heaven]. Let all who desire,[148] ...come."

అം

---

[148] This last line, minus the bracketed words, was the customary announcement in our worship services that we were ready to begin the weekly or monthly communion service—and the invitation for participants to come forward to receive the elements.

## Luke 15:1-3, 11b-32 NRSV

*¹ Now all the tax collectors and sinners were coming near to listen to [Jesus]. ² And the Pharisees and the scribes were grumbling and saying, "This fellow welcomes sinners and eats with them."*

*³ So he told them this parable:*

*¹¹ "There was a man who had two sons. ¹² The younger of them said to his father, 'Father, give me the share of the property that will belong to me.' So he divided his property between them. ¹³ A few days later the younger son gathered all he had and traveled to a distant country, and there he squandered his property in dissolute living. ¹⁴ When he had spent everything, a severe famine took place throughout that country, and he began to be in need. ¹⁵ So he went and hired himself out to one of the citizens of that country, who sent him to his fields to feed the pigs. ¹⁶ He would gladly have filled himself with the pods that the pigs were eating; and no one gave him anything. ¹⁷ But when he came to himself he said, 'How many of my father's hired hands have bread enough and to spare, but here I am dying of hunger! ¹⁸ I will get up and go to my father, and I will say to him, "Father, I have sinned against heaven and before you; ¹⁹ I am no longer worthy to be called your son; treat me like one of your hired hands."' ²⁰ So he set off and went to his father. But while he was still far off, his father saw him and was filled with compassion; he ran and put his arms around him and kissed him. ²¹ Then the son said to him, 'Father, I have sinned against heaven and before you; I am no longer worthy to be called your son.' ²² But the father said to his slaves, 'Quickly, bring out a robe—the best one—and put it on him; put a ring on his finger and sandals on his feet. ²³ And get the fatted calf and kill it, and let us eat and celebrate; ²⁴ for this son of mine was dead and is alive again; he was lost and is found!' And they began to celebrate.*

*²⁵ "Now his elder son was in the field; and when he came and approached the house, he heard music and dancing. ²⁶ He called one of the slaves and asked what was going on. ²⁷ He replied, 'Your brother has come, and your father has killed the fatted calf, because he has got him back safe and sound.' ²⁸ Then he became angry and refused to go in. His father came out and began to plead* with him. [29] *But he answered his father, 'Listen! For all these years I have been working like a slave for you, and I have never disobeyed your command; yet you have never given me even a young goat so that I might celebrate with my friends.* [30] *But when this son of yours came back, who has devoured your property with prostitutes, you killed the fatted calf for him!'* [31] *Then the father said to him, 'Son, you are always with me, and all that is mine is yours.* [32] *But we had to celebrate and rejoice, because this brother of yours was dead and has come to life; he was lost and has been found.'"*

ॐ

# 19.

# Family Business

## Luke 15:1-3, 11b-32 NRSV

It is a story—words from the mouth of Jesus: *"There was a man who had two sons...."* And yet, what Jesus spoke into existence with those words has a substance about it as true and enduring as the real world—our world—the world spoken into existence at the beginning by words from the mouth of God.[149]

*"There was a man who had two sons."*

There was a family. And soon you know that this world Jesus spoke into existence is very much like our own world because there are problems in this family. It is a family that is falling apart.

There is a son in this family who wants out of the family and doesn't care what happens to it when he's gone. "I want out and I'll take *my* share with me!" he says, regardless of the fact that he doesn't technically, or legally, have a share—until his father is dead.

But the father—his father—divides the family property anyway and gives him a share—a son who does not want to be a part of the family.

And if there is property it means that this is not just a family— it is a business. There are assets—resources—whose purpose is to

---

[149] Genesis 1:3, 6, 9, 11, 14, 20, 26.

support the business of the family. It may be no more than a farm, but many people depend on it—for their very lives.

The father is in the business of feeding and clothing and training and protecting all those who make up his "family." And just as they depend on the father to run the business and make sure it is a success, the father depends on his family—and especially his children—to work with him in this family business. Family members work in the family business.

But a son who does not want to be part of his family will not care about the family business, either. The son sells the property out of the control of the family and leaves. He leaves his responsibilities, his home, his family, his father.

The son is not there to do his part and the property the family business depended on is gone, too. A son has deserted the family business. He has declared himself, by his words and by his actions, no son of the family.

But interestingly, his father, who must still run the family business with whatever resources are left, does not respond to this son in kind. The father will not force his son to stay against his will—in the family or in the business. But neither does the father force his son to leave. The son goes on his own—to a far distant country—so far from home that he might as well be—and *may* well be—dead, as far as his father knows.

❧

But this is a father with two sons. His other son is a dutiful son—a diligent son. He is right there with his father every day. He does not demand of his father what he does not deserve. He works as hard in the family business as any hired hand does—and, it turns out, with much the same perspective.

He is seemingly dedicated to the business, but it will soon become apparent that he is no more a part of the family in his own mind than his long-gone brother was. And you do no good for the family business if you are not committed to the family—to being family—because the business of the family is the provision for, and perpetuation of, the family.

Does the father know? Does the father know that he has lost, not one, but both sons? And what does that do to the family business?

The father seems to be the only one in the family who cares about the family business—and the only one in the family who cares about the business of family.

The family business is important, but the business of family is more so. The father never loses sight of the main point: It's all about the family. So look at this family, and learn.

৵৽৻

One son says, in effect: "I am not your son!"

Why would he say that? Is his father unkind? Is his father cruel or unfair?

No. Listen long enough and you learn that the father is just the opposite.

The other son says, in effect, "He is not my brother!"

But when you will not claim your brother, you deny your father as well. "He is not my brother!" is the same thing, in the end, as what the first son said.

The two brothers clearly didn't get along with each other. And the reason is, ultimately, that they did not love their father as they should. If they loved their father, they would love each other to please him. But they don't, and because they don't, neither of the sons comes off looking particularly lovable.

The amazing thing is that while they are "unloving" each other as hard as they can—and therefore, their father, too—their father is doing just the opposite—the opposite of what they're doing and the opposite of what they deserve from him. Their father is loving them even more than they are hating each other.

When the prodigal son returns, broke and broken—humiliated and yet still calculating how to manipulate the old man's compassion—his father throws away his own dignity to restore that wastrel child to the family—and spares no expense to celebrate his return.

When the other son, the supposedly loyal son, berates his father in public for even acknowledging the prodigal's existence, and recites the list of every perceived slight and injustice he has endured at his father's hand, it is the father who has come out to him. It is this remarkable father who continues to love the unloving son, to woo this equally wayward son back into the father's house—back into the family.

And that's how you know that Jesus is talking about a different world.

ംഎ

Oh, we've got plenty of folks like the two sons, crooks and bums and "ladies of easy virtue"—prodigals through and through—and duty-driven legalists, devoid of compassion and determined to get their due as they define it.

But this father who loves them anyway, who will sacrifice himself and everything he has to win them back, who forgives them even before they repent and restores them to places of honor they do not deserve in the family they have rejected—he's from a different world.

This kind of father is from somewhere else. This kind of father is from the world of Jesus. He is a father in a story—a parable—in a world spoken into existence by the words of Jesus.

But is there a "reality" where this father is real? Is there a family created and restored and sustained by this incredible father's love—where the business of this family—led by the father and supported by his children—is the business of turning prodigals and Pharisees into brothers and sisters who love each other as much as their father loves them—who love each other because they have come to understand how much their father loves them and they want to love each other in order to please him?

What if this father was in this world—in this world, but not of this world? What if the unrighteous and the self-righteous of this world could both return to this father and rejoin the family business? What if this is the same Father a twelve-year-old Jesus was referring to when He said He had to *"be about [His] Father's business"*?[150]

❧

The father in the story is a father in a story. But when Jesus tells the story, you know *that* father points to another Father. When Jesus tells a story, there is truth that is truer than true.

In Jesus, a Father has come out to His children who have cut themselves off from His love, who have abandoned their place in the family. In Jesus, this loving, beseeching Father has ignored His eternal glory and divine dignity[151] and come to call us back to the place He has prepared for us in His family and in His family's business.

This Father's first priority is the business of family.

He welcomes the prodigal who will come home—and makes him a son again. He calls the religious—who are offended by His grace and by the unworthy who receive it—to realize that only the unworthy *can* receive it because they alone are offered it. The Father is rebuilding His family by redeeming His wayward children and reconciling them—us—to Himself and one another.

*"There was a man,"* said Jesus, *"who had two sons."*

There is a God Who is enough like that man—that father—that He makes us His children (if we will let Him) after all we've done or failed to do. And He shares the work—the business—of the family with us. It is a dysfunctional family because we are in it. But it is, at the same time, a divine and holy family because the

---

[150] Luke 2:49, KJV.
[151] Philippians 2:6-8.

Heavenly Father has redeemed every one of us and restored us to the family business.

Parable?

Yes.

Reality?

Absolutely!

I'm so glad I'm a part of the family of God![152]

Let's be about our Father's business.

സ-ൈ

---

[152] See Bill and Gloria Gaither, "The Family of God," 1970.

# 20.

# The All or Nothing Gamble

## Luke 16:1-8 ESV

¹ *[Jesus] also said to the disciples, "There was a rich man who had a manager, and charges were brought to him that this man was wasting his possessions. ² And he called him and said to him, 'What is this that I hear about you? Turn in the account of your management, for you can no longer be manager.' ³ And the manager said to himself, 'What shall I do, since my master is taking the management away from me? I am not strong enough to dig, and I am ashamed to beg. ⁴ I have decided what to do, so that when I am removed from management, people may receive me into their houses.' ⁵ So, summoning his master's debtors one by one, he said to the first, 'How much do you owe my master?' ⁶ He said, 'A hundred measures of oil.' He said to him, 'Take your bill, and sit down quickly and write fifty.' ⁷ Then he said to another, 'And how much do you owe?' He said, 'A hundred measures of wheat.' He said to him, 'Take your bill, and write eighty.' ⁸ The master commended the dishonest manager for his shrewdness. For the sons of this world are more shrewd in dealing with their own generation than the sons of light."*

❧❦

Do you like stories?

Most of us do.

133

And what kind of stories do you like? Love stories? Mysteries? Thrillers with unexpected twists?

Whether you prefer to read them, hear them or watch them, if you're like most people, you like stories.

Stories help us make sense of our world and our lives. That's why the Bible is full of them. God wants to help us make sense of the world He created for us—and the unique identities He created in us.

Some of the best stories in the Bible are the ones Jesus tells. We call them parables. And in these stories, there is love and mystery and plenty of those unexpected twists. One of the most mysterious parables of all, at least in terms of why Jesus would tell it, is the one you heard this morning. Jesus tells a story in which a crook is the hero, and, in an unexpected twist, when the crook is at his most deceptive, he is presented as a role model for the followers of Jesus.[153]

❧

The story begins with a wealthy (and therefore powerful) landowner. It seems he has a crooked steward, or manager, working for him. Crooked managers are not unheard of. Corruption in business or government comes to light all the time. And more of it certainly exists that we don't know about.

But, in this case, there's a whistleblower: "Sir, do you know what that manager of yours is doing with your property?"

And, of course, the landowner—the manager's "master"— doesn't know. Or maybe he does know and has been hoping the manager will change. Maybe the master has been waiting to see if the manager will come clean with him and ask for forgiveness. You

---

[153] And again, the historical and cultural details of the setting and the story are drawn from Kenneth E. Bailey's parable studies in *Poet & Peasant and Through Peasant Eyes: A Literary-Cultural Approach to the Parables of Jesus*, Grand Rapids, MI: William B. Eerdmans Publishing Company, 1983, (Book I) pp. 86-118.

see, the master, in this case, is a good and honorable man. He is disposed by nature to be merciful.

But he is also just, and the time has come for justice to be served. The crooked manager's time has run out, and so the master calls him in. When the manager arrives, the green felt is on the long table and court is in session. *"What's this I hear about you?"*

And wouldn't the manager like to know the answer to *that* question!

"He's heard *something*—or I wouldn't be here. What does he know? Does he know everything? Does he believe what he's heard? He must, if he's called me in here like this. What could I say that wouldn't make things worse for me? I've cheated him. It won't help me any to lie to him as well, or argue with him. That would only make him angrier."

§

And so, the crooked manager stands before the employer he has failed and says nothing in his own defense—because he has no defense.

In the silence, the master waits. And the silence grows louder as it grows longer, until it virtually screams the man's guilt—until the master finally breaks the silence—to pronounce sentence on the guilty man: "Turn in your record books. You're fired!"

The words hit him like a physical blow. He staggers out of his master's office. And yet, despite the shock of hearing the verdict, he is also shocked by what he *didn't* hear.

Yes, the master fired him—that's to be expected. But the master did not have him arrested—or beaten. The master did not even scold him or demand repayment. Justice—and mercy. But that's what this master is like.

Everybody knows it. Fair, but generous—that's his reputation (and well earned).

§

But the manager has a big problem. And don't think he isn't working on it.

He thinks: "Okay, I've been fired. What am I going to do? How am I going to live? How am I going to eat?

"Nobody will hire me; I'm a crook. I'm also too weak to do manual labor and too proud to beg in the street. I've got to do *something*! What can I do?"

And then it comes to him. An audacious plan!

"It might not work—probably won't work. But it *could* work. It *has* to work! And besides, it's the only thing I can do."

The manager reasons: "Yes, he fired me, but I still have my freedom. And the master won't be rushing around, telling everybody he fired me. That's not his way. Right now, nobody knows I've been fired. And it takes time to get the record books together. I've got one chance to save myself, but I've got to work fast."

"Hey, kid! Run out and tell all the master's tenants I want to see them right now—in my office."

The clock is ticking. His heart is pounding. But he's got a plan now and it just…might…work.

"Where *are* those guys?!"

Those "guys" are hurrying to the manager's office as quickly as a well-to-do gentleman farmer's sense of dignity will allow. This is not a nickel-and-dime operation we're talking about here. These guys are big wigs in a big business.

And you can hear them thinking: "Most unusual to be summoned like this. What's going on? It must be important. That manager is a piece of work, but he wouldn't call us like this unless the master told him to. And we can trust the master. He's always done right by us—and more. Hope everything's okay. Hope he's got something cold for me to drink after I've hurried like this in this heat."

❧

But when the first man gets to the manager's office, there's neither cold drink nor warm reception.

"How much do you owe my master?" the manager demands.

Confused and offended at this abrupt and disrespectful "greeting," the farmer thinks to himself, "What do you mean, 'How much do I owe?' Everybody knows how much I agreed to pay your boss when the crop comes in."

And getting angry, he snaps back, "Eight hundred gallons of olive oil!"

But the manager ignores his tone of voice and says, "Quick! Sit down! Here's your contract! Change it to 400!"

The farmer's anger is forgotten instantly as he spins around to see the benevolent smile on the manager's face. The manager is about to save him a fortune in rent. The farmer makes the change and the manager reaches for his hand, shaking it and lifting the farmer up out of his seat at the same time. The manager puts his arm around the farmer's shoulder and ushers him to the door with a little wink and a confidential whisper. "I told the master we should give you a break on the rent this year, and you know what a great guy the master is."

"You told him what?!"

But before the stunned farmer can start to thank the manager, he's out the door with a final, "Now, remember who your friends are!" ringing in his ears as the manager grabs the next fellow who's just arrived.

"You! You owe the master how much?"

And the scene is repeated.

The farmers don't stay long in the manager's office, but they do linger long enough outside to compare notes with one another and discover that everybody got the same wonderful break. And then, they start celebrating their good fortune and praising the incredible generosity of the master. The news spreads all over town.

Before long, it reaches the master himself.

And the master realizes he has a choice to make. If he tells the farmers that the manager has tricked them (and him), and that they still owe their full, previously-agreed-upon rents, the celebration will screech to a halt. The joy will turn to resentment—and it won't be directed just at that scoundrel of a manager. The master's reputation as a good and generous man will be destroyed, regardless of the truth.

On the other hand, if he is to maintain his reputation and uphold his position in the community, he will have to pay the price the manager's dishonesty imposed.

And it was just this dilemma that the manager wanted to create when he came up with his "one chance of salvation" plan. He took this audacious action because he thought he knew the master's character well enough to predict which way he would go.

And so, having done his worst—and his best—the manager brings the books he has "cooked" to the master who knows he has cooked them. The manager stands once again before the master who has already judged him guilty, to see if the mercy of this same master will save him from his sins. And the master says to him in rueful admiration: "You are one…clever…crook."

And in that moment the manager knows that he had guessed right—that his all-or-nothing gamble has worked.

೧♦೧

What can you learn from a crook like this manager?

Well, you might learn that you have failed in your responsibility as the agent of God Who is your Master. You know you have failed and God knows it. Don't even bother making excuses; they're useless.

But you have to do something because you're going to lose everything. In fact, there's only one thing you can do: Gamble everything on the mercy of the Master. Believe that (because of His character) He will pay the price Himself of the debt you have incurred. Your debt—not His.

Jesus tells His disciples, "What are you waiting for? Here's a crook who's smart enough to see what is coming and to do something about it. Why shouldn't you be just as smart and just as energetic to bring about the salvation of your eternal soul?"

As a result of his faith in the mercy of his master, the crooked manager is seen in the community as something other than— better than—what he really is. He is welcomed in the house and at the table of those who benefited—unknowingly and innocently— from his quick and clever dishonesty.

As a result of our faith in the mercy of God, we now are welcome in God's house and at His table, despite our sins against Him and our neighbors.

Will you risk everything on God's saving mercy in Jesus Christ?

Judgment is coming and your "books" will be closed.

Will you bet on His grace?

It is the only way.

It is your only hope.

There's not a moment to lose.

Do it now.

ॐ

## Luke 16:19-31 ESV

[Jesus said:]

<sup>19</sup> "There was a rich man who was clothed in purple and fine linen and who feasted sumptuously every day. <sup>20</sup> And at his gate was laid a poor man named Lazarus, covered with sores, <sup>21</sup> who desired to be fed with what fell from the rich man's table. Moreover, even the dogs came and licked his sores. <sup>22</sup> The poor man died and was carried by the angels to Abraham's side. The rich man also died and was buried, <sup>23</sup> and in Hades, being in torment, he lifted up his eyes and saw Abraham far off and Lazarus at his side. <sup>24</sup> And he called out, 'Father Abraham, have mercy on me, and send Lazarus to dip the end of his finger in water and cool my tongue, for I am in anguish in this flame.' <sup>25</sup> But Abraham said, 'Child, remember that you in your lifetime received your good things, and Lazarus in like manner bad things; but now he is comforted here, and you are in anguish. <sup>26</sup> And besides all this, between us and you a great chasm has been fixed, in order that those who would pass from here to you may not be able, and none may cross from there to us.' <sup>27</sup> And he said, 'Then I beg you, father, to send him to my father's house— <sup>28</sup> for I have five brothers—so that he may warn them, lest they also come into this place of torment.' <sup>29</sup> But Abraham said, 'They have Moses and the Prophets; let them hear them.' <sup>30</sup> And he said, 'No, father Abraham, but if someone goes to them from the dead, they will repent.' <sup>31</sup> He said to him, 'If they do not hear Moses and the Prophets, neither will they be convinced if someone should rise from the dead.'"

ॐॐ

# 21.

# Stewardship Matters

## Luke 16:19-31 ESV

Not to put too fine a point on it: Jesus tells a story about a rich man who goes to hell because of poor stewardship.

The old Catholic Bible called the man "Dives" because that's the Latin word for "wealthy."[154] God blessed Dives with lots of money and he spent it all on his personal pleasures: fine clothes, fine foods, gated community. If that's where all his money was going, that's poor stewardship, even if he came up with every penny of it legally and morally.

Dives didn't do what God wanted him to do with his money. And, here as elsewhere, pronouns can be tricky. I just said, "his money." But consider: Is "his" in this case to be understood as Dives', or God's?

Dives, of course, saw it as *his* money, even if he thought God had given it to him—which, as a good Pharisee, was exactly what he would have thought. Deuteronomy 28 says, *"…if you obey…the Lord your God, being careful to do all His commandments…blessed shall you be in the city, and…in the field…"*[155] and everywhere else.

---

[154] The *Vulgate*, a Latin version of the Bible, translated primarily by Jerome, beginning in 382 A.D. It served as the primary Catholic Bible until 1979.
[155] Deuteronomy 28:1-3, RSV.

So, if you're Dives—if you're a rich man—then obviously, God is pleased with you and has blessed you with material prosperity. Take it and celebrate God's generosity and His affirmation of you.

∂❧

But if the money is God's—even *after* God has given it—then your having it may mean something very different. It's like that line from the old hymn,

> "All that we have is Thine alone—
> a trust, O Lord, from Thee."[156]

If God still considers it *His* money, then God probably has some purpose in giving it out as He has—a purpose He expects the fortunate steward *of* His money to carry out *with* the money.

I call the steward "fortunate" because God giving His fortunes to people *is* a sign of His divine favor; it is a blessing. And many good people will get rich because they are good—because righteousness, by its very nature, rewards the one who is righteous. And though the reward of righteousness is not *always* financial in nature, it often is.

But the good fortune of prosperity is not that being wealthy enables the recipient of God's material blessings to live "the good life," defined materialistically.

Rather, the good fortune is that God has chosen to enable you to participate in—and contribute to—*His* good work. The more you have, the more you are able to do those things that have the greatest significance and value in God's eyes—and that bring the greatest satisfaction and joy, not just in the moment, but for all time.

∂❧

---

[156] See the hymn, "We Give Thee But Thine Own," by William Walsham How, 1868.

142

Which demonstrates more respect and the greater value—the owner of a huge business giving you some free samples, or his setting you up as a partner in the business, with all the resources you need to be breathtakingly successful?

God does not give out product samples—courtesy souvenirs. He supplies significant resources for producing all the company's finest goods and services.

Dives spent his (or His) fortune on fine food, fine clothes, a fine house—and a fine funeral, no doubt.

And then, according to Jesus, there was hell to pay.

Stewardship matters, it seems, in the kingdom of God—and a lot more than you might imagine.

ॐ

## 2 Corinthians 5:14-21 ESV

[14] *For the love of Christ controls us, because we have concluded this: that one has died for all, therefore all have died; [15] and he died for all, that those who live might no longer live for themselves but for him who for their sake died and was raised.*

[16] *From now on, therefore, we regard no one according to the flesh. Even though we once regarded Christ according to the flesh, we regard him thus no longer. [17] Therefore, if anyone is in Christ, he is a new creation. The old has passed away; behold, the new has come. [18] All this is from God, who through Christ reconciled us to himself and gave us the ministry of reconciliation; [19] that is, in Christ God was reconciling the world to himself, not counting their trespasses against them, and entrusting to us the message of reconciliation. [20] Therefore, we are ambassadors for Christ, God making his appeal through us. We implore you on behalf of Christ, be reconciled to God. [21] For our sake he made him to be sin who knew no sin, so that in him we might become the righteousness of God.*

ॐॶॖ

## Luke 18:9-17 ESV

[9] *[Jesus] also told this parable to some who trusted in themselves that they were righteous, and treated others with contempt:* [10] *"Two men went up into the temple to pray, one a Pharisee and the other a tax collector.* [11] *The Pharisee, standing by himself, prayed thus: 'God, I thank you that I am not like other men, extortioners, unjust, adulterers, or even like this tax collector.* [12] *I fast twice a week; I give tithes of all that I get.'* [13] *But the tax collector, standing far off, would not even lift up his eyes to heaven, but beat his breast, saying, 'God, be merciful to me, a sinner!'* [14] *I tell you, this man went down to his house justified, rather than the other. For everyone who exalts himself will be humbled, but the one who humbles himself will be exalted."*

[15] *Now they were bringing even infants to him that he might touch them. And when the disciples saw it, they rebuked them.* [16] *But Jesus called them to him, saying, "Let the children come to me, and do not hinder them, for to such belongs the kingdom of God.* [17] *Truly, I say to you, whoever does not receive the kingdom of God like a child shall not enter it."*

෨෧

# 22.

# Reconciliation

## 2 Corinthians 5:14-21, Luke 18:9-17 ESV

So, here's the picture: Two guys—maybe strangers to each other, maybe not—both happened to head to church about the same time. One is unusually well dressed; the other, not so much.

Maybe the place is crowded, and they end up next to each other, though they would rather not be. Everybody is praying out loud, since silent prayer hasn't been invented yet or something, and the two men next to each other are joining in the din with their own personal prayers.

The well-dressed man is well-dressed because he is a tax collector. He can buy the best clothes because he takes what money he wants from his neighbors. The other man clothes himself in the simple, but distinctive, style of the spiritually superior Pharisee. If clothes *don't* "make the man," they still can give you a pretty good idea of the kind of man you're dealing with.

The well-dressed man is praying, but it's the other guy, the one in the simple clothes, who's turning up the volume and turning heads. And for a personal prayer, he's spending an awful lot of time telling God about the guy next to him. To hear the Pharisee's prayer—and he's going to make sure that everybody within yards *will* hear it—to hear his prayer, the guy standing next to him in the very nice clothes is such a very bad guy that he ought to be tossed out of God's House on his ear—or on the seat of his high-priced and well-pressed pants.

But the guy with the impressive suit isn't there to show off his wardrobe. He doesn't seem to be paying any attention to the guy beside him who's paying so much attention to him.

The guy praying loudly next to him isn't too happy about being next to him. But the guy in the good suit doesn't seem to be too happy, either. And the reason seems to be that he has the same opinion of *himself* that the man beside him does.

The well-dressed guy is going to wrinkle his suit coat because, while he's praying, he keeps hitting himself in the chest. And he keeps repeating, over and over: *"God, be merciful to me, a sinner!"*

The "praying P.A. system" standing next to him is telling God something a bit different, "God, You are so lucky to have a 'sin avoider' like me on Your team!"

And then, these two guys—maybe strangers, maybe not—head home after praying their hearts out.

One was begging for reconciliation—one was bellowing for recognition. Both, it turns out, got what they prayed for. But sooner or later, both men will understand that reconciliation with God is a lot better purpose for prayer than the recognition of men.

⤜⋙⋘⤛

The Apostle Paul had been one of these plain-dressing, proud-praying Pharisees[157] before he got his understanding about prayer and everything else "adjusted" on the Damascus Road.[158]

When Paul (on the way to his appointment to persecute the followers of Christ) encountered the Christ he thought was dead (and found that He was very much alive), Paul experienced a reconciliation with God he didn't even know he needed. Paul's

---

[157] Galatians 3:4-5.
[158] Acts 9:3-6.

relationship with God had been broken when he thought it was perfect.

Then, before he had a chance to beg for mercy, he received mercy. Before he could do anything to make things right with God, God made Paul right with Him.

Paul became the poster child for divine reconciliation. Paul no longer lives for himself.[159] He's no longer impressed with himself. He looks at himself differently. He looks at everybody else differently. He looks at Christ differently because he doesn't have a choice. He met Christ face to face and Christ wasn't dead the way Paul thought He was.

Christ showed Paul how different everything is because of what God did in Christ. And Paul was reconciled. He was reconciled to God, and he concluded that what God did for him in Christ God did for everybody else in Christ, too. Paul concluded that God was reconciling the whole world to Himself in Christ, and that anyone who was "in Christ" was reconciled to God.

And so he made it his business from then on to get people "in Christ" so that they would, in fact, be reconciled with God. It became his obsession—his ministry. It was his message to a world of people who had no clue they needed to be reconciled to God— or if they did, they had no clue—no correct clue—about how to go about getting reconciled—how it could be accomplished for them...

...which is understandable, since reconciliation is one of the hardest things in the world for anybody to accomplish—with anybody. Paul was reconciled to God, but he was constantly trying to bring about reconciliation with other people. Sometimes, he was mediating between other people, such as Philemon and his runaway slave, Onesimus,[160] or Euodia and Syntyche, two "church

---

[159] Galatians 2:20.
[160] Philemon 1:8-21.

ladies" in the Philippian church who were on the outs with each other for some reason.[161]

As often as not, Paul was trying to pull off some reconciliation between himself and some church—or some faction in a church—he himself had founded. That's really what's going on in 2nd Corinthians. The Corinthians have given Paul the cold shoulder and he's trying to work out a reconciliation with them by pointing to the reconciliation he and they have both received from God.

"If God would reconcile us to Himself, can't you—shouldn't you—reconcile me to yourselves? Isn't this what God wants you to do? Isn't this what your reconciliation with God is for?" writes Paul.

৯•৯

But, oh, how hard it is for people to get along—even good, Christian people like us. Oh, we expect it to be hard for nation to be reconciled to nation. We have multitudes of professional diplomats—ambassadors—all around the world, and their best efforts frequently can't even keep the peace, much less make peace when it's been lost. It's hard for individuals—strangers—to get along. It's hard for neighbors. It's hard for schoolmates and siblings and spouses to get along—and harder still to be reconciled when we've had some falling out.

But if I am reconciled to God through the death of Christ—and you are reconciled to God through the death of Christ—can we not be reconciled to one another through the death of Christ as well? Is this not, perhaps, God's will for His children—that reconciliation might be the result in all our relationships?

To hear Paul tell it, reconciliation is our business. It's the job God has given us. Not that we could die on the Cross like Jesus did—not that we could pay the price to reconnect some sinner to God—ourselves or anybody else.

---

[161] Philippians 4:2-3.

But we can tell people about this reconciliation with God. And we can urge people to let God reconcile them to Himself. We can pray prayers for the divine reconciliation of others and prayers that God will reconcile people with each other. And we can recognize that because we have been reconciled to God, God can and does enable us to be reconciled to others.

Have you been reconciled to God?

Then you have been appointed a minister of reconciliation—an ambassador carrying a sacred message of peace to anyone in the world who can't get along with God. To fulfill your mission, you must let God reconcile you with those in your home, your family, your neighborhood, or your school, who are distant, hostile, estranged.

Hard to do?

In many cases, humanly impossible.

৯–৩

But suppose those two men who went to pray that day had stood next to each other and prayed the *same* prayer—not the Pharisee's prayer that put more distance between himself and the man beside him—and the God above him—but the tax collector's prayer, humbling himself to the point that God had to come closer just to hear him make his confession and repent his way to reconciliation.

Jesus said it was *that* man who went home "justified" (another word for "reconciled"). Two praying the tax collector's prayer would have come away from the experience, not further apart, but united in heart and mind, and pure in spirit—as pure as the little children who came to Jesus to be blessed.

We are not those little children, but we are made like them by Christ—as are any we bring to Christ for reconciliation through His death.

Get the message? Be reconciled to God—and to each other.

৯–৩

## Luke 19:1-10 ESV

¹ *[Jesus] entered Jericho and was passing through.* ² *And behold, there was a man named Zacchaeus. He was a chief tax collector and was rich.* ³ *And he was seeking to see who Jesus was, but on account of the crowd he could not, because he was small in stature.* ⁴ *So he ran on ahead and climbed up into a sycamore tree to see him, for he was about to pass that way.* ⁵ *And when Jesus came to the place, he looked up and said to him, "Zacchaeus, hurry and come down, for I must stay at your house today."* ⁶ *So he hurried and came down and received him joyfully.* ⁷ *And when they saw it, they all grumbled, "He has gone in to be the guest of a man who is a sinner."* ⁸ *And Zacchaeus stood and said to the Lord, "Behold, Lord, the half of my goods I give to the poor. And if I have defrauded anyone of anything, I restore it fourfold."* ⁹ *And Jesus said to him, "Today salvation has come to this house, since he also is a son of Abraham.* ¹⁰ *For the Son of Man came to seek and to save the lost."*

ॐ

# 23.

# How a Little Man Grew Up

## Luke 19:1-10 ESV

According to the children's song, "Zacchaeus was a wee little man"—or, to be politically correct, we might just say he was "vertically challenged."

And don't think he didn't know it! The biggest thing to happen in Jericho since "the walls came a tumblin' down,"[162] and Zacchaeus can't get past—or see past—the mob of onlookers, to get a glimpse of this new religious Rock Star named Jesus.

Can you visualize it? Frustrated and fuming, Zacchaeus grabs up the skirts of his resplendent robe and runs down the road, ahead of the parade, to a sycamore fig tree. Then he pushes his equally resplendent hat back on his head and grabs a tree limb, pulling himself up with determination, though not nearly the speed and agility he displayed the last time he climbed a tree, years ago as a boy. And when he reaches a suitable vantage point, he settles himself in with as much dignity as he can muster—which is none, really—and awaits the approaching commotion.

---

[162] See Joshua 6:1-20, and the African-American spiritual, "Joshua 'Fit' the Battle of Jericho," based on that passage.

When the procession gets to him, Zacchaeus has an excellent view of something he didn't expect to see. The Jesus Zacchaeus wanted to get a look at has stopped right under his tree and is looking right back up at Zacchaeus. In fact, everybody is looking at Zacchaeus, the little man, perched like a parrot, up there on a limb. Everybody is looking somewhere—everybody is seeing something—but you would be surprised at all the different things they see.

Zacchaeus sees, once again, the problem with being physically small. In his mind, he wouldn't be in this ridiculous predicament if he were taller. Some of our modern translations say Zacchaeus was "a short man." The actual Greek phrase is "little in stature." And, with your permission, I would like to shift to that term.

It has to gall Zacchaeus to be little in stature. He has a big job and a big bank account. He has a big influence in Jericho and he lives big. He is a big man in so many ways. It has to gall him to be a little man, physically.

The citizens of Jericho, the people who pay Zacchaeus their taxes and feel his influence, look up in that tree and see a man who is little in other ways, too. There is a verse at the end of the second chapter of Luke's Gospel that says, *"Jesus increased in wisdom and stature, and in favor with God and man."*[163]

The same cannot be said for Zacchaeus, as far as the gawking crowd is concerned. The little man everybody is looking at is a little man in all the ways that count, no matter how big he has made himself in all the ways that don't.

Zacchaeus is a little man when it comes to wisdom. He has been clever and calculating. He has broken the code on how to build up a big business. He has brilliantly pursued a course that ultimately leads nowhere good. And there he is, a pathetic figure, out on a limb, in more ways than one. He has not increased in wisdom.

---

[163] Luke 2:52.

Zacchaeus is a little man spiritually. He is a Jew, a son of Abraham like all the rest, but day after day, year after year, he has traded his glorious heritage, his special relationship with God, for personal privilege and financial favors. Yet all of those favors are as nothing in comparison to the favor of God. In that, Zacchaeus has not increased. He is a little man spiritually.

And why does everybody—save One—delight in the sight of the little man's discomfort?

Because he is a little man in their eyes. They do not respect him. They do not like him. They do not accept him as one of them. He has traded his identity as one of the community for the alienation and isolation that comes with making himself big at their expense. Though he could have, and should have, he has chosen *not* to increase in favor with man. Zacchaeus is a little man.

The scene is so symbolic: Zacchaeus looks down on everyone from the elevated, yet isolated, vantage point he has attained. But even there, he is a little man who will, sooner or later, have to come down—or fall down—from his perch. There he is: Zacchaeus, the little man who wants to be big—but isn't.

❧

Of course, Zacchaeus isn't the only one. You may be one of those people who did everything you could think of to become a "big" person. You may have a lot of big achievements in your career. You may have gotten a big position in a big organization with big responsibilities and a big budget. You may have a big personality or a big ego.

But if you did not increase in godly wisdom—if you did not grow up spiritually and morally—you may be suffering from the same "Little-Person Syndrome" as Zacchaeus.

But I'm not here to taunt you or take pleasure in your predicament. I have suffered from the same syndrome. I've climbed that same tree—and still find myself grabbing its branches from time to time. The point is not what the people see when they look at little Zacchaeus. The point is what Zacchaeus sees—and hears—and experiences—at the biggest moment in his little life. Zacchaeus is about to find out how a little man grows up.

ঌ৵৽

Everybody is looking at Zacchaeus, but the only One Zacchaeus sees is Jesus. What everybody else sees is no longer important to Zacchaeus; it only matters what Jesus sees. And what Zacchaeus discovers is that he is not too little for Jesus to see him. Jesus does not ignore him or "be-little" him. Jesus comes to where he is and looks at him.

Have you ever thought, "Jesus is looking at me"? Did you ever realize as you went about all the big things you invested your life in that Jesus was constantly coming right where you were—that He was looking right at you? And that *His* measure was—*is*—the only measure of "little" and "big" that matters?

Everything that Zacchaeus did to make himself a big man only made him a little one.

Jesus looks up in the tree and sees this little man, and because Jesus looks with the eyes of God and sees the substance of God— the image of God—still there in little Zacchaeus, He calls him down out of the tree and down from the inflated image Zacchaeus had created for himself.

"Zacchaeus! Come down immediately! Come down out of that tree and come down from all the big façades you've erected to make yourself look big. Right now, you're a little man—but all that can change."

Zacchaeus sees the eyes of Jesus on him and hears the words of Jesus to him, and he responds obediently and immediately, glad to be the focus of Jesus' attention, and glad to give up his self-selected, elevated position. Isn't it interesting that it isn't until Zacchaeus comes back down to earth and puts his small stature face to face with Jesus, that he finally has a chance to grow up?

Jesus confronts Zacchaeus in his high and mighty condition and then Jesus goes home with him. *"Zacchaeus, I must stay at your house today!"*

Jesus has to stay at Zacchaeus' house? Why? The necessity is certainly not Jesus'. Jesus could stay anywhere—or nowhere. Jesus knows what it's like to have no place to lay His head.[164]

No, Zacchaeus is the one who must have Jesus stay at his house. When Jesus comes into a little person's home, and stays in that home, that little person starts to grow up.

Watch! The little man will become a big man because Jesus comes into his home.

ॐ∽

Little Zacchaeus marches home with Jesus at his side, the crowd parting in amazement before them and then flowing back together to follow along behind. The little man throws Jesus a big party—he has the bankroll to do it. Jesus and His disciples recline on the plush couches—probably the first guests whose friendship Zacchaeus hasn't purchased with patronage or "payola."[165]

Everybody else watches from the open windows and doorways. But everybody else is starting to look a little smaller. They don't like Zacchaeus and they don't like Jesus liking Zacchaeus. They've taken the measure of Zacchaeus and put him in the "little man" category, and that's where they mean for him to stay—which, under the circumstances, is kind of "small" on their part.

But Jesus ignores them and concentrates on Zacchaeus. Luke doesn't tell us what Jesus says, but at some point in the discussion, Zacchaeus stands up and calls Jesus, "Lord." And the little man, who had devoted his life to becoming the lord of all he surveyed, all of a sudden looks a lot bigger.

---

[164] Luke 9:58.
[165] The term "payola" has come to mean the payment of a bribe to get someone to do what he or she would not be inclined to do otherwise.

*"Here and now,"* he tells Jesus, *"I give half my possessions to the poor. I will make every wrong right—and more!"*

And the moral midget has been transformed before their eyes into a giant of generosity. The little body now holds a boundless soul. The big ego has been replaced by a bigger spirit of self-sacrifice in the service of the One Who emptied Himself of everything anyone would consider "big,"[166] in order that He might be the biggest Servant of all[167]—the Savior of all.[168]

The One Zacchaeus now calls "Lord" takes the measure of Zacchaeus and declares him a big man. *"This man is a true son of Abraham!* This man has increased in favor with God and with man."

ॐ

Who doesn't want to be big? Every little person wants to grow up. But you can't make yourself a big person, no matter what you do, unless, of course, you look to Jesus and come down off your lofty perch as He commands you, and go with Him where He leads you, and get out from under all the big things that stunt your moral and spiritual growth.

It's a funny thing—almost as funny as a little man scrambling up a tree: Come to Jesus "big" and He will make you "small." But come to Him "small"—humble and repentant—and He will make you "big," in every way that matters.[169]

You heard what He said, this Jesus: *"The Son of Man has come to seek and save the lost."*

Here He is. Come down, little one, and He'll help you grow up.

ॐ

---

[166] Philippians 2:6-8.
[167] Matthew 23:11.
[168] 1 John 4:14.
[169] Matthew 20:16.

# 24.

# A Different Point of View

## Luke 19:1-10 ESV (p. 152)

Most of the time in the Gospels, you get to look at things through the eyes of Jesus. But as Jesus approaches the city of Jericho on His way to His rendezvous with the Cross, Luke provides us a different point of view. Luke tells us what Jesus is looking at, but the focus is on what someone else sees.

That "someone" is a man named Zacchaeus—"a wee little man," as the song goes.[170] If you lived in Jericho, you would probably have seen Zacchaeus as a little weasel, or a big crook, or even a huge traitor. He was a Jew who collected taxes for the harsh and hated Romans—and he collected enough extra to make himself rich in the bargain. Whenever they saw Zacchaeus, the Jewish residents of Jericho "saw red…"

…which was too bad, in a way, because Zacchaeus was really something of a comic figure. A runt of a man, Zacchaeus tried to compensate for his physical shortcomings with all the accoutrements of material success.

But it didn't work. He was what he was: a little man.

---

[170] "Zacchaeus Was a Wee, Little Man," traditional Christian children's song.

Even when he climbed up in a tree in his expensive clothes to catch a glimpse of this Jesus character, the citizens of Jericho could have seen how silly he looked. But, instead, they could only see the guy who was robbing them blind—and doing so "legally." In the end, the important thing is not what they saw, but what Zacchaeus saw—and what happened to him as a result.

Zacchaeus was willing to look silly—this time, at least—to get a look at Jesus. That was his point of view. He probably knew he looked silly; most people know when they do. But, in this case, it was worth the embarrassment to get in a position to see this Guy everybody was hearing and talking so much about. Zacchaeus put himself in a vulnerable position in relation to Jesus—and it changed his life.

Zacchaeus wanted to see Jesus and did what he had to do to make that happen. And when Zacchaeus saw Jesus, he found himself confronted by a Person Who was not willing to let Zacchaeus remain an unengaged bystander. When Zacchaeus saw Jesus, Jesus called him—by name—and offered—demanded—to go home with him.

What Zacchaeus saw from a distance made him want to see more. What he saw of Jesus close-up made him want Jesus in his home. When Zacchaeus took Jesus home, and experienced a relationship with Jesus, he wanted—and found that he was able—to be a different person—a person made over in the image of Jesus.

Zacchaeus saw Jesus and saw that he, Zacchaeus, needed to be—and could be—a different person. Jesus gave Zacchaeus a different perspective on himself, his possessions and his place in the community. Jesus gave Zacchaeus a divine perspective, and a divine imperative to subordinate himself to Jesus.

Why would Luke make Zacchaeus the central figure in this story? Why is the point of view of Zacchaeus so important?

Perhaps it's because there are a lot more people who need to see what Zacchaeus saw, first in Jesus, and then in themselves in relationship with Jesus.

If Zacchaeus started out as the comic figure of a little man, he ended up—by the grace of God and his relationship with Jesus Christ—with the noble and generous character of a giant man of faith. Zacchaeus saw what everyone needs to see, and he adopted the point of view that salvation requires.

Jesus told Zacchaeus and his neighbors, *"The Son of Man came to seek and to save the lost."*

Zacchaeus saw that.

Do you?

ॐ

# 25.

# What Happened at Jericho

## Luke 19:1-10 RSV

The text for tonight's sermon is found in the 19<sup>th</sup> Chapter of the Gospel of Luke, and we will be reading it in just a moment.

But before we do, I want to recall for you something our pastor[171] pointed out several months ago in a sermon about understanding scripture. He said that one of the basic principles of biblical interpretation is that "scripture interprets scripture."

One of the simplest interpretive tools is *context*. Looking at what comes before or after a passage can provide a deeper perspective than the passage alone might suggest. For instance, in Luke 18, the chapter before tonight's text, Jesus tells parables about hard-to-find justice and a hard-to-believe tax collector.[172] He encounters a rich man who wants what money cannot buy and a blind beggar who just wants to see the light.[173] Jesus tells the disciples and the other Passover pilgrims traveling with Him how

---

[171] I was "filling in" for the pastor of a church in Alexandria, Virginia, where we were members while I was serving in an administrative position in Washington, DC.

[172] Luke 18:1-8; 18:9-14.

[173] Luke 18:18-23; 18:35-43.

to enter God's kingdom,[174] while He Himself is preparing to enter Jerusalem, God's holy city, where men will seize Him, torture Him, and kill Him[175]—and call it "doing their religious duty."

But before they get to Jerusalem, there is Jericho.

ॐॐ

Over a thousand years before Jesus enters the city, his Old Testament namesake, Joshua, led Hebrews warriors around it and saw God break down its mighty walls.[176] Some walls are going to come "tumblin' down" in the *New* Testament Jericho as well, the day Jesus comes to town.

In the time of Jesus, Jericho is an important place. King Herod had made it his winter capital. It is a fortified military outpost, guarding the Jordan Valley approaches to Jerusalem against attack.[177] That there is danger around is no secret; Jesus based the parable He told about The Good Samaritan[178] on well-known fact.

The wealth that flows through the city of Jericho attracts a lot of people. It attracts the vicious bandits hiding in the mountains. It attracts poor beggars like the blind man sitting beside the road. And it has attracted a little fellow named Zacchaeus.

Perhaps I should clarify that just a bit and call Zacchaeus a *short* fellow, because what the Bible actually says is that he is "small of stature." In fact, he is quite a *large* presence in these parts—he is the *chief* tax collector. He *owns* the "franchise." He *runs* the operation that takes money from the Jews and gives it (or a lot of it, at any rate) to the Romans occupiers.

Zacchaeus *is* "the law" when it comes to taxes. The first commandment in Zacchaeus' law is: "Satisfy the Romans." And

---

[174] Luke 18:17.

[175] Luke 18:31-33.

[176] Joshua 6:1-20.

[177] See Ehud Netzer, "The Winter Palaces of the Judean Kings at Jericho at the End of the Second Temple Period," *Bulletin of the American Schools of Oriental Research*, No. 228 (December 1977), pp. 1-13.

[178] Luke 10:25-37.

the second is like unto it: "Make Zacchaeus rich!" Zacchaeus has obeyed *his* law to the letter, just as the rich man in the previous chapter claimed to have done with *God's* law. Zacchaeus is now a rich man. He is "a man to be reckoned with."

But on the day Jesus comes to town, Zacchaeus—for all his wealth and power—is, in one important way, not much different from the blind beggar outside the city gate: He wants to see—and can't.

Let's see what happens in Jericho:

ॐ—ॐ

*¹ [Jesus] entered Jericho and was passing through. ² And there was a man named Zacchae'us; he was a chief tax collector, and rich. ³ And he sought to see who Jesus was, but could not, on account of the crowd, because he was small of stature. ⁴ So he ran on ahead and climbed up into a sycamore tree to see him, for he was to pass that way. ⁵ And when Jesus came to the place, he looked up and said to him, "Zacchae'us, make haste and come down; for I must stay at your house today." ⁶ So he made haste and came down, and received him joyfully. ⁷ And when they saw it they all murmured, "He has gone in to be the guest of a man who is a sinner." ⁸ And Zacchae'us stood and said to the Lord, "Behold, Lord, the half of my goods I give to the poor; and if I have defrauded any one of anything, I restore it fourfold." ⁹ And Jesus said to him, "Today salvation has come to this house, since he also is a son of Abraham. ¹⁰ For the Son of man came to seek and to save the lost."*

ॐ—ॐ

What you see happening here in Jericho, of course, depends on your perspective. We *usually* look at events in the Gospels from the perspective of Jesus, which is certainly what the writers mean for us to do, since, by definition, the perspective of Jesus is the right and proper one.

But it is not the only one presented; there are others. This is not to say that every perspective is right, or fair, or honorable, or of equal value. Not every set of eyes will see things accurately. But everybody has a perspective, a vantage point, and we may be able to appreciate the perspective of Jesus that the Bible presents us better if we are at least familiar with the other choices available.

So how do we get a different perspective?

The media people have developed a neat trick in recent years that you see in movies and commercials. Someone told me it's called "freeze-frame" photography. Some dramatic action is taking place and, all of a sudden, the action stops, and the still picture rotates right before your eyes so that you are positioned for a different look—a different perspective—when the action resumes.

Suppose we were to stop the action and rotate the picture on this scene in Jericho. Suppose, for instance, we were to find ourselves, not looking over the shoulder of Jesus, but packed tightly in the crowd looking *at* him. Suppose we were looking at what is happening in Jericho from *their* perspective? What would it look like then?

❧

We'll come back to that, but let's rotate the picture a little more just now, till we find ourselves clinging tightly to the branches of a sycamore tree, not looking through the eyes of Jesus at a little man out on a limb, but actually looking through the eyes of this Zacchaeus—at a Jesus Who is looking back at him.

Zacchaeus wants to see Jesus, but we do not know if he wants to see God. Consider his perspective. Zacchaeus is successful, powerful, wealthy—and frustrated. Luke says *"He seeks to see who Jesus is, but can't, on account of the crowd."* He just wants to see Who Jesus is. There are no newspapers in Jericho—no TV. They don't have high-speed internet service yet. There are no photographs of Jesus, and probably no religious book stores to market them. No one is painting His picture—not yet anyway. Just think: No one who hasn't seen Jesus in person knows what He looks like.

But *news* about Him has spread all over the place.[179] Word of what He's done—and said—has been carried by eyewitnesses along the way from village to village, where others have picked up the stories and passed them on farther still. (Anyone who makes the oppressive power structure uneasy is worth talking about.)

And now this mysterious, exciting Stranger is coming to Jericho, according to the pilgrims on the road: "Jesus, the Galilean prophet, is coming! He's right behind us!"

So Zacchaeus figures this Jesus is worth a look. But people are in the way. You and I can understand *that* perspective. Around here, people are *always* in the way when you want to do something. It's just "a given."

And Zacchaeus has to be careful. His "work," and the success he's had in it, have made it none too safe to mingle with people. It might not be a smart move to dart into the crowd and try to shove his way to the front. But Zacchaeus is determined and clever. He anticipates, and takes advantage of, emerging opportunities. He always has. This approach to life has made him rich and powerful. But it hasn't made him safe in a crowd. So this short man climbs a tree to get a little perspective.

Zacchaeus went looking for Jesus, but I don't think he ever imagined that Jesus would come looking for him. Zacchaeus sees Him, all right, and hears Jesus call him down out of the tree. Amazing things happen when you look at the Jesus Who's looking at you. As the song says:

> "Turn your eyes upon Jesus.
> Look full in His wonderful face,
> and the things of earth
> will grow strangely dim,
> in the light of His glory and grace."[180]

May I offer you my perspective?

---

[179] Matthew 4:24; 9:31; Mark 1:28; Luke 7:17.
[180] Helen Howarth Lemmel, "Turn Your Eyes Upon Jesus," 1918.

I see Zacchaeus as a "prodigal son," in a way.[181] In his own way, he had said to his Heavenly Father: "Give me my share of the property that belongs to me (and let me do with it what I want)!" And God gave him the inheritance due every child of Abraham— a spiritual heritage greater than gold—a priceless place in the community of faith—and he *squandered* it in loose living among foreigners.

And one day, he woke up to find himself morally bankrupt and cut off from his own people. He had "made his bed"—in this case, in a most luxurious pigsty—and then resigned himself to lie in it, because, unlike the prodigal in the parable, he could see no way to do otherwise. Zacchaeus has reached the top of his profession, the top of the economic and political ladder—and the top of a sycamore tree—only to discover that he has hit bottom in the eyes of God and man.

And then Jesus comes to Jericho and looks up at him in that tree—and calls him.

What is happening at Jericho?

The Heavenly Father has sent His Son, Jesus Christ, to seek and save this lost child—this poor, spiritually-prodigal son— because, like the rich young ruler in the previous chapter, all his vast worldly gain turns out to be useless for filling his deep emptiness—worse than useless, because his human power and earthly wealth are consuming the life that God wants to redeem.

What is happening at Jericho?

Jesus is reaching up into that tree and plucking Zacchaeus out of that handcart he is going to hell in and putting him on the train that's bound for glory.

"Zacchaeus, hurry up and get down here, because I'm going to spend some quality time with you today."

---

[181] Luke 15:11-24.

And Zacchaeus jumps down—or climbs down as quickly as his stubby legs can manage, or falls down in shock, and *"receives him joyfully,"* according to Luke.

Here again, perspective is important. For instance, we don't know *why* Zacchaeus is so joyful. Is he excited by this unexpected public recognition? Is he pleased at the aggravation this will certainly cause all the people in the crowd who hate him? Is he looking forward to impressing Jesus with sumptuous hospitality fit for a king?

We don't know, but we can guess.

Anyway, Jesus calls him out of the tree and goes to his house.

And between verses 7 and 8, some time passes.

◈◈

We don't know exactly what the perspective of Zacchaeus is when he ushers Jesus into his home, but we do know that what is said between them that Luke does *not* record is nevertheless *not* said in secret. That's not how things are done in Jericho, or anywhere else in that part of the world. When somebody special comes to dinner, the doors and windows of the house are thrown open and the townspeople crowd around and watch the show.

We also know that, at some point in the conversation between Jesus and Zacchaeus, this chief tax collector—this "robber baron of revenue"—has an incredible change of perspective. When he responds to the call of Jesus and invites Him, first into his house, and then into his heart, the world changes for this wealthy runt.

Jesus comes to Jericho and brings salvation. But there's more. This salvation stimulates a response of restitution, justice and charity in Zacchaeus. Consider the ripple effect when the chief tax collector gets a moral makeover from the Messiah. Because of what happens to Zacchaeus, the economic realities in Jericho will change—as will politics and the whole structure of society.

What's happening at Jericho?

A town is getting a foretaste of the Messianic Banquet.[182]

But not everybody is finding it to their liking. If Jesus' perspective is right, the kingdom of God isn't at all what the fine folks of Jericho have been expecting. The very last person in Jericho anyone would have thought of as worthy to enter the kingdom of heaven is, in fact, the very first granted admission. If Jesus is right, the crowd has the wrong perspective.

But we need to rotate the picture again, and have a look from their perspective, just to see what they see, and why.

಄಄

As you stand in the crowd, you first experience a cynical delight at the ridiculous image of that despicable little Zacchaeus dangling from a tree limb as this charismatic, holy Man approaches. Then, you feel confusion and disapproval as Jesus stops and calls him down and walks him back to that fancy mansion built with the money his henchmen collected (stole) from you and your neighbors as "taxes."

Is Jesus *endorsing* Zacchaeus and his evil ways, his ill-gotten gain, the great hurt and injustice he's done to most—if not all—the locals in the crowd? Why is Jesus honoring him this way? Zacchaeus doesn't *deserve* it! Whose side is Jesus on, anyway?

಄಄

Jesus brings salvation to Jericho—to Zacchaeus' house. But the truth is that not everybody wants Zacchaeus saved. You see, when God changes the world of Zacchaeus, He changes everyone else's world in Jericho as well. He shakes up the status quo for a community grown comfortable with its hatred and bitterness toward this extremely "hate-able" little man. And a lot of people are not happy that Jesus is "setting Zacchaeus free."

Is this a warped perspective?

---

182 Matthew 22:2.

Yes, but it's not unique.

In the novel, *King Rat*,[183] James Clavell writes about allied soldiers in World War II forced to "live like rats" in the inhuman brutality of a Japanese POW camp. The central character is an unscrupulous Corporal King who runs a black market in the camp. The corporal controls every aspect of their lives, making him the de facto ruler of these wretched men—their "King Rat." His fellow prisoners resent the power he wields over them, even as they submit to his corrupt system to get the barest necessities of life. When the camp is finally liberated after the Japanese surrender, the "King Rat" becomes just one more prisoner set free. His power disappears the instant the gates of their "hell" are opened.

One man had steadfastly refused to "do business" with the "King Rat." Lieutenant Grey, the Provost Marshal, or Police Chief, among the captives, was obsessed with catching him and seeing him punished, but he never succeeded. Even their liberation did not weaken Grey's bitter determination to make Corporal King pay for his crimes in captivity. As they prepare to leave the camp, another officer urges Grey to give up his grudge and enjoy the fact that they have survived their "hell" and are free men again. The story concludes with Grey rejecting the idea with a startling and cynical admission about his relationship with the "King Rat": "I stayed alive by hating him."

If a troublemaker ever changes, all the victims have to "shift" as well. Living with a "new" Zacchaeus (their former "King Rat") will not be easy for the people in the crowd who have proudly and passionately hated him until now—until Jesus comes to town—and makes something miraculous happen in Jericho.

কে‑ঙ

What is *your* perspective on how God deals with the Zacchaeuses in *your* world? You know God cares about the most

---

[183] James Clavell, *King Rat*, New York, NY: Little, Brown and Company, 1962.

despicable sinners around you, the people who've caused you the most pain or loss or aggravation. God is always out to redeem them, to forgive them, to save them and transform each of them into somebody totally different. You know He is, because *Jesus* is, and Jesus says He and His Father *"are one."*[184]

Which of your enemies will Jesus cross the path of this week? And what will you do or say or think if you are there when it happens?

The crowd's perspective?

"Sinner!"

But Jesus says, "Saved!"

And what about the "Zacchaeus" in *us*?

Oh, it may not be *all* of who we are. It may just be some small, seemingly insignificant part of our personalities. But is there not some secret place inside committed to getting ahead, regardless the cost—to getting our own way, at whoever's expense? And don't you know, that's exactly where Jesus is going to pause on His way through our lives, and look us in the eye and say, "Come down from there right now. I need to talk to you about this."

What happens when Jesus comes your way? Because you know He does, every day, time and again.

そ๑ふ

So maybe it's time to rotate the picture one more time, back to the perspective we started with—back to the perspective of Jesus.

In the end, Zacchaeus is everything the crowd knows him to be and hates him for being. Zacchaeus knows what he is as well, and how they feel about him. And while Jesus knows all this, too, He knows something else—something more. He knows what God can—and what God wills to—make of one like Zacchaeus. The visit with Zacchaeus is not a detour for Jesus; it is the purpose for the journey.

---

[184] John 10:30.

Isn't it ironic that Zacchaeus would climb a tree so that he could see the Jesus Who is on His way to Jerusalem—to climb His own tree—so that He can save all the Zacchaeuses of the world?

"*...when I am lifted up from the earth,*" Jesus says, "*[I] will draw all men to myself.*"[185]

Now, that's a perspective!

"Come down here, Zacchaeus, I mean to change your life—and Jericho—today. Come down, Zacchaeus, and be saved."

∂∽∾

---

[185] John 12:32, RSV.

## Luke 21:5-9 ESV

⁵ *And while some were speaking of the temple, how it was adorned with noble stones and offerings, [Jesus] said,* ⁶ *"As for these things that you see, the days will come when there will not be left here one stone upon another that will not be thrown down."* ⁷ *And they asked him, "Teacher, when will these things be, and what will be the sign when these things are about to take place?"* ⁸ *And he said, "See that you are not led astray. For many will come in my name, saying, 'I am he!' and, 'The time is at hand!' Do not go after them.* ⁹ *And when you hear of wars and tumults, do not be terrified, for these things must first take place, but the end will not be at once."*

ॐॐ

# 26.

# What Will Be the Sign?

## Luke 21:5-9 ESV

I go back to my hometown from time to time. The house I grew up in—the house my father built for his mother, "Momma Hill"—belongs to someone else now. The "church" I grew up in is abandoned. The congregation bought another building in the suburbs some years ago and relocated there. The city closed my high school when the shrinking number of students in town forced them to consolidate. The parking lot is empty; the classrooms quiet.

When I was young, these places were the center of my life. They had always been there. I never imagined at the time that would ever change. But so much of what I knew then is gone.

৵৽৾৾

Jesus was having a conversation with some fellows in the Temple. The Temple was the crown jewel of Jerusalem. They say the gold that adorned its walls shown like the sun, and the stones were so white they looked like snow. The Temple towered over everything else in the city that towered over everything else in the countryside as far as the eye could see. It was a wonder of the world.[186]

The Temple was built to last forever, but Jesus said the day was coming when every one of those dazzling stones would be knocked down. The idea was incredible, as you can tell from the response Jesus got from those He was talking to.

"When? How will we know? What will be the sign?"

But what is prophecy in the mouth of Jesus is history as Luke records the story a few decades later. The first readers of the Gospel of Luke already knew that the Temple had been destroyed, just as Jesus predicted. And they knew when and how the stones had been knocked down. And looking back, they knew the signs of its destruction, as only Jesus knew them looking forward.

It is easy to see the signs of something after the fact. But to see the signs along the way, that's something else again. For the longest time, I am told, there were no signs here in Pinehurst—no street signs. The attitude seemed to be: "If you didn't know where you were going, you shouldn't be trying to get there!" Those with the benefit of past experience knew the "signs"; those looking into the "unknown" ahead—especially in the dark—did not.

"When is this Temple—this marvelous Temple—going to be destroyed?" they ask. "What is the sign?"

And Jesus answers them with an answer that seems to be no help at all. "Whenever," He says. "Doesn't matter, really. But it's going to happen, regardless."

And it won't be the first time.

Six hundred years before Jesus stood in the Temple and predicted its destruction, the prophet Jeremiah was standing in the same place and making the same prediction about the first Temple on the site[187]—the Temple built by King Solomon. Jeremiah got into almost as much trouble as Jesus did for what they said,[188] but

---

[186] Simon Goldhill, *The Temple of Jerusalem*, Harvard University Press, 2005, p. 1.
[187] Jeremiah 7:1-15.
[188] Jeremiah 11:18-19.

because the prophet was not crucified, he lived to see the stones of the Temple he knew knocked down[189]—just like Jesus predicted of the stones of the Temple built in New Testament times.

You see, Jesus isn't concerned about time tables, because He knows something His audience apparently doesn't: "The time will come when your Temple will be destroyed." Temple of Solomon—Temple of Herod—it doesn't matter. Temples will be destroyed. They built great temples in Jerusalem, and every one of them was destroyed.

But this truth is not limited to the temples the Jews built. Everybody built temples in the ancient world. And the day came when all of them were destroyed. The time will come when *your* temples will be destroyed, too.

What do I mean?

Think about what a temple is. A temple is a sanctuary—a place of security. It is a monument, a place you consider holy, a place where you worship, where you bring your valuable offerings.

People build temples to many gods. You can build a temple to your health or your career—to your family or your financial security or your independence. You can build a dazzling monument with all the appearances of permanence. You can expect it to last forever. But the day will come when every temple will be destroyed.

What will be the sign? The sign is already here. The sign is you.

You are a finite creature living in a world marked for destruction. *"In the world, you will have tribulation,"*[190] says Jesus. "Your temples will be destroyed."

"Upstairs. Downstairs. We all fall down!"[191]

---

[189] Jeremiah 52:12-23.

[190] John 16:33, ESV.

[191] One of several variations of the final two lines of the children's nursery rhyme, "Ring Around the Rosie." Some traditions locate the origin of the verse to the time of the Great Plague of London in 1665 and 1666.

In this world, sooner or later, not one stone will be left on another. Every monument you erect will come down. Look at all the things and people in your life that are gone already. The rest is but a matter of time.

What will be the sign?

You are the sign.

෬෧

But there is another sign—a Sign, not of destruction, but of victory—a Sign that has and will change the world.

It was the evening of the 27th of October in the year 312. The Roman Emperor Constantine, preparing for battle, saw a vision in which he was told, "In this sign, you will conquer." He painted the sign he saw on the shields of his soldiers and won the battle. The sign of his victory was the sign of the Cross.[192]

And with that victory began the conversion of Constantine to Christianity, and with his conversion, the acceptance of Christianity in his empire, from which came its preeminence in Europe and its propagation in America, and your opportunity to hear the gospel and respond in faith.

Now we sing, "Lift High the Cross,"[193] because the sign of destruction in us has been overcome by God's Sign of salvation.

But here, we must make a distinction. The Cross is not the Sign of salvation; it is only the symbol of the Sign. Just as the sign of destruction is human; so is the Sign of salvation—human *and* divine.

Paul said, *"For as in Adam all die, so in Christ all will be made alive."*[194] If you are the sign of your destruction and that of all you hold dear in this world—all your temples—so Jesus, the Man Who hung on the Cross, is the Sign of the power that overcomes this

---

[192] Lactantius, *On the Deaths of the Persecutors*, before 325 A.D., and Eusebius, *Life of Constantine*, Book 1, before 339 A.D.

[193] George Willian Kitchin, "Lift High the Cross," 1887.

[194] 1 Corinthians 15:22, NIV.

coming-apart world. *"In this world, you will have tribulation"*—you will see your temples destroyed—*"but be of good cheer,"* He said, *"I have overcome the world."*[195]

Jesus stood in the Temple of Jerusalem and predicted—accurately—that the Temple would be destroyed. That got His listeners' attention. But He said something else in the Temple they couldn't figure out at all. *"Destroy this temple,"* He said, *"and in three days, I will raise it up."*[196]

The people who heard Jesus say this were completely baffled. The people who read about it in the Gospel understood perfectly. They didn't have to wonder about the sign. The temple He spoke of was His body. And after Jesus was raised from the dead, His disciples remembered what He said.[197]

The temples of this world will be destroyed—it's the nature of this world. But there is a temple *"not made with hands, eternal in the heavens."*[198] The Bible says that, in the heavenly city, the Lord God Almighty and the Lamb Who is Jesus Christ are its temple.[199] It's going to be a whole lot different there—no destruction there. That temple will last forever.

But there's one more thing we need to say about this business of temples and the signs about them. Or one more thing the Bible needs to say. Paul wrote, *"Don't you know that you yourselves are God's temple and that God's Spirit dwells in your midst? …God's temple is sacred, and you together are that temple."*[200]

And then Paul wrote, *"you are…built on the foundation of the apostles and prophets, with Christ Jesus Himself as the chief cornerstone. In Him, the whole building is joined together and rises to become a holy temple in the Lord.*

---

195 John 16:33, RSV.
196 John 2:19, RSV.
197 John 2:21-22.
198 2 Corinthians 5:1.
199 Revelation 21:22.
200 1 Corinthians 3:16-17, NIV.

*And in Him, you, too, are being built together to become a dwelling in which God lives by His Spirit.*"[201]

The Sign of Jesus overcomes and nullifies your sign. His salvation overcomes and nullifies your destruction. In *this* world, not one stone will be left on another in the temples we revere. In *that* world, not one eye will ever shed a tear. In *this* world, everyone will know tribulation. In *that* world, no one will suffer or grieve or die.[202]

When I was growing up, I did not realize that the temples that seemed so permanent would one day be destroyed. I know now they will be, because so many have been already.

But I also know that the destruction of this world is being overcome by the salvation of the next, and every time a temple of this world is destroyed, I am drawn deeper into that other temple, where Jesus Christ is the Cornerstone and His Spirit dwells in me.

If I am the sign of the destruction of this life, watching the destruction of everything around me, and waiting for my own demise, Jesus is the Sign of my salvation, in this world and the next.

What will your sign be?

ॐ‧

---

[201] Ephesians 2:19-22, NIV.
[202] Revelation 21:4.

# 27.

# What a Development!

## Luke 23:32-43 ESV

*32 Two others, who were criminals, were led away to be put to death with [Jesus]. 33 And when they came to the place that is called The Skull, there they crucified him, and the criminals, one on his right and one on his left. 34 And Jesus said, "Father, forgive them, for they know not what they do." And they cast lots to divide his garments. 35 And the people stood by, watching, but the rulers scoffed at him, saying, "He saved others; let him save himself, if he is the Christ of God, his Chosen One!" 36 The soldiers also mocked him, coming up and offering him sour wine 37 and saying, "If you are the King of the Jews, save yourself!" 38 There was also an inscription over him, "This is the King of the Jews." 39 One of the criminals who were hanged railed at him, saying, "Are you not the Christ? Save yourself and us!" 40 But the other rebuked him, saying, "Do you not fear God, since you are under the same sentence of condemnation? 41 And we indeed justly, for we are receiving the due reward of our deeds; but this man has done nothing wrong." 42 And he said, "Jesus, remember me when you come into your kingdom." 43 And he said to him, "Truly, I say to you, today you will be with me in paradise."*

ॐ—ॐ

Who was it who used to say, "What a revoltin' development *this* is!"?

I thought it was Jimmy Durante; it turned out to be William Bendix in *The Life of Riley* show on radio and TV.[203]

The phrase popped into my head one morning this week as I was thinking about this thief on the cross next to Jesus.

Yes, I grant you, it's an absurd comparison. When the character Chester A. Riley said the line on TV, it always got a lot of laughs. Getting crucified, on the other hand, is no laughing matter.

So maybe it was that I hadn't had my breakfast yet or wasn't quite awake. My mind wasn't really focused the way it usually is when I've gotten myself organized for the day. But I've learned not to discount those thoughts that come before I'm ready to start thinking. I've learned that maybe I ought to think them through. So let me think this one through with you.

What is a thief on a cross going to *say* during the endless, agonizing hours he is hanging there, stripped of everything— including dignity, sanity and hope?

You can scream out your pain. You can spit out curses on your killers—and everybody else, for that matter. You can beg for the mercy no one will give you.

But if you could think clearly enough, for a second, to consider your situation, you might just think, "What a revoltin' development *this* is!"

Riley used to get himself in trouble. He set himself up for disaster all the time with his bumbling around and listening to his neighbor's bad advice. But he never got in a bind like this one the thief is stuck with. This truly is revoltin'.

ॐ

But there *is* a connection between Chester A. Riley, the fictional buffoon, and the unnamed, unknown thief on the cross.

---

[203] *The Life of Riley* aired on radio from 1944 to 1951, and on television from 1953 to 1958.

Both are spared the disastrous consequences that seem certain to follow on their self-inflicted dilemmas.

It's absurd; but it's there.

The thief looks over at the Man suffering and dying like him on the cross beside him and sees something that tells him the Man is *not* suffering and dying like him. That Man, Jesus, is suffering and dying in a totally different way—and for a totally different reason.

It's absurd, but the thief sees that it's true.

And then this pathetic, dying wretch of a man—this thief—does something absurd. He prays to the Man on the cross beside him. No eloquence. No lofty, liturgical phrases. There's no time or strength left for that. Just a desperate request. One prayerful petition: "Remember me. *Remember me when You come into Your kingdom.*"

It's absurd to pray like that. It's absurd to think that a Man on a cross could be a king.

It's absurd to think that He'll come into a kingdom or anything else after He dies—except a common criminal's grave.

And then the Man dying on a cross between two thieves utters an even more absurd response: *"This day you will be with Me in paradise."*

No doubt, everybody standing around watching got a laugh out of that: "Yea, let's see *that* happen."

છ⊸త

And here's the really funny thing—funny absurd, not funny to laugh at—except that the funny thing is so absurdly wonderful that if you were the thief who prayed the prayer, you would certainly laugh out loud for joy: The Man on the middle cross turned out to be, not merely a king, but *the* King—the King of kings—and Lord of lords.

This kingdom the thief wanted to be remembered in turned out not to be one of *"the kingdoms of this world,"*[204] but a heavenly kingdom that encompasses this and every world in all Creation. And the suffering of that thief who prayed to Jesus from his cross turned out to be not worth comparing with the glory that was revealed to him at the end of this, his last and worst day—and, ultimately, best day—on earth.[205] The paradise of Jesus turns out to be even better than "The Life of Riley."[206]

৯•৯

People liked to listen to and watch Chester A. Riley because he was sort of an "everyman." We ought to look at and listen to the thief on the cross for the same reason: He is every one of us.

We are suffering and dying—victims of our own moral bumbling—waiting without hope for the disastrous consequences to come—unless, in a moment of sanity, we pray that the King Who was crucified for us will remember us, after all.

No matter what you do with your life, it will never, ultimately, be more than "a revoltin' development."

But when you call upon the King—when you see the situation for the hopeless mess it is and do the only thing you can, and pray—the most absurdly wonderful development of all takes place: Paradise with Jesus.

Who was it who said to Jesus, *"Remember me when You come into Your kingdom"*?

I hope it was you.

৯•৯

---

[204] Revelation 11:15, KJV.

[205] Romans 8:18.

[206] This phrase seems to have originated in Ireland where, at one time, the O'Reilly clan became so powerful that they minted their own money, and people who had a lot of their coins were said to be "living off their 'Reillys.'"

# From the Acts of the Apostles

## Acts 1:1-11 ESV

*¹ In the first book, O Theophilus, I have dealt with all that Jesus began to do and teach, ² until the day when he was taken up, after he had given commands through the Holy Spirit to the apostles whom he had chosen. ³ He presented himself alive to them after his suffering by many proofs, appearing to them during forty days and speaking about the kingdom of God.*

*⁴ And while staying with them he ordered them not to depart from Jerusalem, but to wait for the promise of the Father, which, he said, "you heard from me; ⁵ for John baptized with water, but you will be baptized with the Holy Spirit not many days from now."*

*⁶ So when they had come together, they asked him, "Lord, will you at this time restore the kingdom to Israel?" ⁷ He said to them, "It is not for you to know times or seasons that the Father has fixed by his own authority. ⁸ But you will receive power when the Holy Spirit has come upon you, and you will be my witnesses in Jerusalem and in all Judea and Samaria, and to the end of the earth." ⁹ And when he had said these things, as they were looking on, he was lifted up, and a cloud took him out of their sight. ¹⁰ And while they were gazing into heaven as he went, behold, two men stood by them in white robes, ¹¹ and said, "Men of Galilee, why do you stand looking into heaven? This Jesus, who was taken up from you into heaven, will come in the same way as you saw him go into heaven."*

৯–৩

# 28.

# You Will Be Witnesses

## Acts 1:1-11 ESV

The Church—the community of those who believe that Jesus is the Savior sent from God—was born in the presence of Jesus, in the relationship He established with His first followers who responded to His teachings and witnessed His death and resurrection. The Gospels don't say much about the Church, but they do record Jesus saying, *"...I will build my church...."*[207] And even this brief phrase reveals three critical truths about the Church.

The Church is the possession of Jesus Christ. It is His possession in its total global form as the community of all believers everywhere. It is His possession in its congregational form as a formal, local organization of believing members. And it is His possession in every interaction of any number of Christians—even as few as two—under any circumstances. The Church, in all its aspects, is His. It—we—belong to Him. We may belong to a church—to *the* Church. But no church—not even ours—belongs to us. It is His Church.

And His Church must be built—and it *will* be built. You and I are very concerned about building a church building. We are

---

[207] Matthew 16:18, ESV.

frustrated by the obstacles we have encountered. We are anxious about all the practical and financial details that must be dealt with. We want to "build our church."

But far more important than the "brick and mortar" that will go into a physical facility somewhere around town is the building of the spiritual edifice that we are and are to be. You must be built up as a believer, individually. You are to be a solid building block, a substantial part of the whole. And we must be built up together as a strong spiritual structure, firm in faith, love and loyalty to Christ and each other.[208] We are *His* Church. We must be—and will be—built.

❧

And Jesus Himself will build us: *"I will build my church,"* He said. Jesus was building His Church every day of His ministry, with every parable He told and every miracle He performed. He was building His Church as He suffered on the Cross[209] and as He rose from the grave.[210] He was building His Church when He confronted Thomas[211] and when He commissioned those who were present when He ascended into heaven.[212]

And He has been building His Church ever since, even as He is doing here today.

Right now—right here—Jesus your Savior is building you—us—His Church. He was building yesterday. He will be building tomorrow—and the day after—and every day after that—until He comes back to earth the same way He went into heaven.[213] Jesus will always and forever build His Church.

---

208 Ephesians 2:19-22.
209 John 19:25-27.
210 Matthew 28:1-10.
211 John 20:19-31.
212 Matthew 28:19-20.
213 1 Thessalonians 4:16-17.

That's the story the Book of Acts was written to tell. It is the story of that early Church—that first Church. But it is also, in some way, the story of all the churches Jesus is building—all of the churches that belong to Him. It is our story—and an exciting one—because His building of His Church never ends.

And how does Jesus build His Church? How does He build believers and congregations and the world-wide family of faith?

The blueprint for His building is in the passage we heard today.

ॐ∘ॐ

The Bible says: *"He presented Himself alive to them by many proofs."* And Jesus is building His Church today by presenting Himself alive to people by many proofs.

How does that song go?

"I serve a risen Savior. He's in the world today.
I know that He is living, whatever men may say.
I see His hand of mercy. I hear His voice of cheer.
And just the time I need Him, He's always near."[214]

Jesus is presenting Himself to you, alive, by many proofs—in you and around you. And what do you say?

"He lives! He lives! Christ Jesus lives today!"

And you, my friend, are being built by Jesus as part of His Church.

ॐ∘ॐ

How does Jesus build His Church?

The Bible says: He speaks of the kingdom of God. He spoke to His first followers in person. He speaks to you in the record of what He said to them. He speaks to you in the words of dedicated and inspired teachers and preachers and writers—and in the hallowed thoughts of your heart. Jesus tells you of the glorious things that are now yours through His atoning sacrifice and God's

---

[214] Alfred Henry Ackley, "He Lives," 1933.

incredible mercy. He reveals the realities of a realm where the God Who died for you is your eternal sovereign Lord.

"He walks with me and talks with me
along life's narrow way."[215]

❧❦

How does Jesus build His Church?

The Bible says: He promises and provides Holy Spirit power. Jesus said, *"Before many days, you will be baptized with the Holy Spirit… you will receive power when the Holy Spirit comes upon you…."*

You may not think much of yourself as a building block in the Church Jesus is building. But you need to understand that Jesus is not building His Church with you as you are—He's building with you "treated"—"reinforced."

Lumber is good. *Treated* lumber is better. Concrete is good. *Reinforced* concrete is far better. You are being "treated" with the Holy Spirit. You are being infinitely strengthened by the Holy Spirit Whose power is reinforcing every aspect of your spirit.

❧❦

How does Jesus build His Church?

The Bible says: He appoints witnesses—people who have seen Him and heard Him and experienced the power He gives, who go and point to the Jesus they have seen alive—who go and repeat the sacred words they have heard Jesus say—who go and offer the divine power they have received from Jesus.

Jesus told those who sat through His Sermon on the Mount[216]—and those who served five thousand souls the feast Jesus furnished from a few loaves and fish[217]—those who ran away when the mob hauled Jesus away from Gethsemane,[218] that they

---

[215] Ackley, ibid.
[216] Matthew 5—7.
[217] John 6:1-13.
[218] Mark 14:48-50.

would receive power and be His witnesses. They would be the materials and the tools with which He would build His Church.

And they were—as you will see in the weeks to come.

But you, too, are the material Jesus is using to build His Church—the Church He is continuing to build today. And you are the instrument He intends to use—that He has prepared for His use—as He builds.

You—all of you—have received power.

You—all of you—are His witnesses.

You—all of you who have seen Jesus alive and heard His holy Word—have been built—are being built—into His Church.

And you will yourselves help Jesus build His Church. You are His witnesses—in this town and this county—in this country and to the ends of the earth.

Jesus is building His Church—with you.

☙❧

## Acts 2:36-42 ESV

[Peter said:]

 ³⁶ *"Let all the house of Israel therefore know for certain that God has made him both Lord and Christ, this Jesus whom you crucified."*

 ³⁷ *Now when they heard this they were cut to the heart, and said to Peter and the rest of the apostles, "Brothers, what shall we do?"* ³⁸ *And Peter said to them, "Repent and be baptized every one of you in the name of Jesus Christ for the forgiveness of your sins, and you will receive the gift of the Holy Spirit.* ³⁹ *For the promise is for you and for your children and for all who are far off, everyone whom the Lord our God calls to himself."* ⁴⁰ *And with many other words he bore witness and continued to exhort them, saying, "Save yourselves from this crooked generation."* ⁴¹ *So those who received his word were baptized, and there were added that day about three thousand souls.*

 ⁴² *And they devoted themselves to the apostles' teaching and the fellowship, to the breaking of bread and the prayers.*

ॐ⊸ও

# 29.

# Know For Sure

## Acts 2:36-42 ESV

You might think that this is the kind of information you would just as soon not know.

Knowing it—that they were responsible for killing Jesus—and that Jesus was really their long-promised and deeply-desired Messiah—and God Himself—made the Jews listening to Peter on Pentecost less than "happy campers." It "cut them to the heart." You might think they could have gone all day—all their lives, in fact—without knowing it, and been perfectly happy.

But it turns out that, sometimes, what you don't know *can* hurt you. Badly. Eternally.

There are some things that you don't know that you need to know—you need to know them if you know what's good for you. There are some things you need to know—for sure.

The sermon Peter preached at Pentecost is about something everybody needs to know for sure.

అంజ

First, you need to know the bad news—that *you* bear some of the responsibility for torturing to death the one Man out of all humanity Who was God incarnate.

But maybe you don't know that. Maybe you think you're not responsible.

"*I* wasn't there! *I* wasn't even born! *I* wouldn't have been a part of that even if I had been alive and there. *I* know *I* didn't crucify Him!"

And yet, you need to know—for sure—that you did. You need to know that your sin—your sinful nature and your sinful deeds—caused the Crucifixion of Jesus just as much as the Jewish leaders who contrived it[219] and the Roman officials who committed it[220] and all the rest of us—every person in the history of the world who ever lived long enough to sin. God had to come and become Jesus and die because of every one of us.[221]

As hard as it is to face, you need to know it—and know it for sure. Just like you need to know for sure that this Jesus Who died on the Cross was God Himself in human flesh,[222] serving as the Messiah He had promised the Jews for centuries that He would send to them to save them from their suffering.[223] God came to earth Himself to keep His word to His people. They killed Him— we killed Him—but it was still Him Who became Jesus, and—as Jesus—was and is—God and Savior.

They didn't want to know it. Maybe you don't want to know it. But Peter knew it and knew everybody else needed to know it, too. And by the time he was done telling them what they needed to know, 3,000 of them, at least, did know it.

❦

And because they knew the bad news, they were finally in a position to know the good news. Know for sure you crucified Jesus—but know for sure as well that Jesus is Lord and Christ—

---

[219] John 11:45-53.
[220] John 18:28—19:34.
[221] Romans 3:10, 23.
[222] John 1:14; Colossians 1:15-20.
[223] Isaiah 11:1-9; Micah 5:2-4.

God and Savior. Jesus is just as much God and just as much Savior after the Crucifixion as before.

How do you know? How did Peter and the others know?

They saw Jesus alive *before* the Crucifixion. They saw Jesus dead *as a result of* the Crucifixion. They saw Jesus alive *after* the Crucifixion. When you spend time with Somebody Who's been raised from the dead, you know some things—for sure.

So Peter has let them—us—know the bad news, and within it, the (as yet unseen) seed of some very good news.

❧⋅❦

*"What shall we do?"* they say, which is another way of saying, "We know that we don't know what we need to know."

When you know there is something you very much need to know—even if you do not yet know what it is—you know a lot more than when you didn't think you needed to know anything.

It is a dangerous arrogance that thinks there is nothing one needs to know. It is a healthy humility that asks the question that is asked of Peter.

And Peter tells them what else they need to know. *"Repent,"* he says, *"and be baptized every one of you in the name of Jesus Christ for the forgiveness of your sins."*

Peter knows about repentance. You would know quite a lot about repentance if you were a close friend of Jesus who denied and deserted Jesus in the hours before His execution.[224] So, yes: *"Repent."*

And just as John the Baptist called sinners to a baptism of repentance in the Jordan[225]—just as Jesus commanded His disciples to make other disciples and baptize them[226]—so Peter lets his listeners know that baptism is to be their sacred symbol of their saving knowledge of Jesus Christ.

---

[224] Matthew 26:69-75.
[225] Matthew 3:1-6.
[226] Matthew 28:19-20.

And then Peter lets them know something else: *"You will receive the gift of the Holy Spirit."* You who crucified the Man Who was God and Christ will receive the Spirit of God when you repent of your part in the killing of the Christ—when you repent of the sins for which God came and died on that Cross.

Now we're getting to some good news—great news—worth knowing. And it gets better still.

Did you know that you are not the only one who, despite your sins, can know the forgiveness of God and the intimate presence of His Spirit with you and within you?

According to Peter, *"The promise is for you and for your children and for all who are far off, everyone whom the Lord our God calls to Himself."*

And did you know that when Peter says the promise is *"for all who are far off,"* he probably doesn't mean just people who live a long way from Jerusalem, but those who lived a long time before that Pentecost and those who will live a long time after.

*"Those who are a long way off"* may also refer to people who are so bad that neither they nor anybody else can imagine God forgiving them and letting them get close to Him. What must it be like for the worst person in the world to come to know that forgiveness and the promise of the Holy Spirit is for him—or her—too? And to know how to receive them?

A hundred and twenty people knew the risen Christ before the day of Pentecost and the outpouring of the Holy Spirit. That's understandable. You know what His life and death and resurrection mean if He was telling you what it all meant before He died and reminding you what it means after He has been raised. You know what He wants you to do for the same reason.

And by nine a.m., on Pentecost, you also know that you *can* do it, even though at one time you knew for sure you couldn't. When you are awash in the power of the Holy Spirit, you will always know things you didn't know—just like He promised you you would.

❧

But then, 3,000 people come to know this Crucified and Risen Lord and Christ—3,000 people who didn't know Him before that day. And thousands more come to know Him in the days that follow. And most of these never saw Jesus during His ministry—never heard Him speak—never witnessed a miracle at His hand. He never appeared to them physically, risen from the dead. And yet, they came to know, for sure, that He was exactly Who Peter said He was.

And now that number has grown to billions—multitudes the world over—and you, if you know Him.

But how could they know Him? How can you know Him today, for sure, with little more than these same words of Peter to go on? How do those who know Jesus know that they know?

All you need to know is there in the story we heard today. Peter told them what they needed to know. And *"with many other words he bore witness and continued to exhort them."* So they came to know more.

*"And...those who received his word were baptized,"* which meant they also repented of their sins. And because of that they knew God's forgiveness. And they knew the gift of the Holy Spirit.

And it says, *"they devoted themselves to the apostles' teaching and the fellowship, to the breaking of bread and the prayers,"* which means their Lord and Christ made Himself known to them, in the breaking of bread as He had in Emmaus after His resurrection,[227] and in their times of fellowship, fulfilling His promise to be in the midst of even two or three of them.[228]

And just as He revealed the meaning of the scriptures to His disciples after the Resurrection,[229] so those who believed in Jesus came to know Him better and better as they studied the scriptures about Him with their spiritual leaders. And in the prayers, including

---

[227] Luke 24:28-35.
[228] Matthew 18:20.
[229] Luke 24:27; 44-45.

the special one He taught them,[230] they came to know Him Who heard all their prayers.[231]

How can you know for sure that God has made Jesus both Lord and Christ?

You can't—unless you believe what the eyewitnesses have told you about the bad news of the gospel—and the good news that comes out of it.

You can't know Jesus with certainty unless you do what the Bible tells you to do: Repent, be baptized, receive God's forgiveness and the gift of the Holy Spirit, be received into the body of believers and devote yourself to the daily disciplines of your relationship with Jesus, such as scripture reading, fellowship, communion and prayer.

You cannot know *about* Him for sure. But you can know Him with an unwavering certainty, if you give yourself to Him, committing yourself to live—with Him and in Him—every day.

Until you do, you'll never know.

❧

---

[230] Matthew 6:9-13.
[231] 1 Peter 3:12.

# 30.

# And Then What?

## Acts 2:42-47 RSV

*⁴²And they devoted themselves to the apostles' teaching and fellowship, to the breaking of bread and the prayers.*

*⁴³And fear came upon every soul; and many wonders and signs were done through the apostles. ⁴⁴And all who believed were together and had all things in common; ⁴⁵and they sold their possessions and goods and distributed them to all, as any had need. ⁴⁶And day by day, attending the temple together and breaking bread in their homes, they partook of food with glad and generous hearts, ⁴⁷praising God and having favor with all the people. And the Lord added to their number day by day those who were being saved.*

❧

We heard the end of Acts, Chapter 2 read earlier in the service. The beginning of that chapter is all about Pentecost. As Baptists, we're big on Pentecost. For us, Pentecost is the coming of the Holy Spirit 50 days after the Resurrection. On Pentecost, the Holy Spirit unleashed the disciples from their fears and led them out into the world to preach the gospel boldly to thousands of people. When you want to emphasize saving souls, you go to Acts, Chapter 2, and preach about Pentecost.

And then what?

Pentecost is a hard act to follow: a 10-day-long prayer meeting, roaring winds inside a locked room, tongues of fire and foreign language fluency without the benefit of a Berlitz course. Peter preaches one sermon and thousands of people sign up for membership.

What do you do for an encore after that?

Or more importantly, what do you do with the people after you've gotten them to give their hearts to Jesus?

What did the church do with all these new believers after Pentecost? What do we do, as the church, after we're saved?

There's Pentecost, but what then?

❧

After describing what happened at Pentecost, Luke offers a snapshot of the early church: *"They devoted themselves to the apostles' teaching and to the fellowship, to the breaking of bread and to prayer."* That's not a bad template for what a church—a body of believers in Jesus—ought to be doing, even today.

A lot of churches these days are doing a lot of things, many of them useful—some of them appropriate. But I suspect if they're not focusing on these things—the apostles' teaching, fellowship, communion and corporate prayer—they're missing something vital as a church. And whatever else they are, they won't be healthy spiritually, which is the only measure that really matters for the body of Christ.

Notice what's not in this template: ministry programs, personal quiet times or evangelism. Oh, these things come later, for sure. But they're not the first things.

First, there is Bible study, fellowship, communion, and worship—all group activities—all things the believers do together.

How does a church get its act together?

If the church formed on Pentecost is any example, a church gets its act together by getting its people together.

Now here's where it gets tricky, because we Baptists have made showing up every time the church doors are opened the measure of true godliness. If we are to be martyred for our faith, we are much more likely to be crucified on a clock than a cross. The more time you spend at church, the better your Christianity must be.

I don't think that's what Luke is trying to say.

These people—these new Christians—and the "older" Christians, the disciples—were determined to spend time together—not just to *be* together—but to *do* certain things together. They became what a church is supposed to be by doing these things together. They became what they were supposed to be by devoting themselves to the apostles' teaching, to fellowship, to the breaking of bread and the prayers.

౸⋅⋖

Let's consider why Luke would list these four things as what these people devoted themselves to do together.

Consider the apostles' teaching. The apostles are the people who know what Jesus said and did. To our knowledge, Jesus never wrote anything down. The only way for believers to know what Jesus said and did was to have somebody who heard what He said, and saw what He did, tell them. And this is what the apostles, the Twelve, do. Some of the apostles' teaching will become the New Testament in later years as the apostles, or others who hear them, finally write down what the apostles have said.

The Pentecost church needs to hear the stories of Jesus and their explanations while they're together because everyone needs to hear the same thing at the same time, so they can ask questions and clarify, so they will share a common understanding of the good news and of the gospel's claim on their lives. And anyway, the apostles don't have time to tell everyone individually.

The Word of God presented through the disciples revealed God's redemptive purpose and His sacrificial plan, carried out by Jesus. The New Testament does the same thing for us today. This word of God through the apostles also defined these early Christians as a group that was *in* the world but no longer *of* the world.[232] The world can no longer provide these Christians an identity that is acceptable to them or God. And that hasn't changed.

When the members of a church do not study the Word of God together, each will study it individually—or not at all. The one way allows you to distort the gospel to fit God into your personal preferences; the other way leads to sons and daughters of God who have no clue who they are or how God desires them to live. Better that we study together and keep each other "honest to God."

❦

As for fellowship: It's not just about enjoying the company of other Christians. When you've spent years and years together, it's not unusual to feel comfortable in one another's company. But these people in Jerusalem on Pentecost are strangers to each other.

And the term used here for "fellowship" means much, much more than just "hanging out" together. Luke chose a Greek word, "*koinonia*," that means "sharing life." In their daily fellowship, they were taking a chance on each other for the purpose of breaking down barriers. They were bearing one another's burdens, solving one another's problems, meeting one another's needs—because they were now "family."

When we recognize that we are sinners, we recognize that we are, as a result, brothers and sisters. They discovered through the gospel that they had been "together" in their sinfulness. Now, as the church, they understand they are "together" in the salvation they have been provided, completely by grace, in the person of Jesus Christ.[233]

And so are we.

---

[232] John 17:16-18.
[233] Ephesians 4:4-6.

These people—these church people—studied the gospel together. They shared their lives.

৵৽

And they broke bread together. They shared in communion as we did a moment ago.

Have you ever thought about the fact that you don't take communion alone? That guy beside you is the church—that lady over there, too. That's why I had you all wait to eat and drink: so that we could do it together.

In some churches, they used to practice "closed communion"—that's c-l-o-s-e-d—"closed communion." If you weren't a member of that particular congregation, you didn't qualify to "commune" at the table of our Lord.

The early church took a little different approach. Take the "D" off *closed* communion and you get the early church version. They practiced "c-l-o-s-e"—"close" communion. They got together every day. They met in each other's houses and broke bread together. They shared meals and communion, which was only natural, because by breaking bread together, they demonstrated and experienced the "sacred significance of a shared meal."

The Lord's Supper was the symbol of the sacrificial death of Jesus Christ that set them free from sin and death, and every meal they shared together as "Jesus believers" was a symbol of the Lord's Supper.

Teaching, fellowship, breaking bread…

৵৽

…and prayer.

Luke says, they were devoted to "the" prayers. That definite article in front of the word "prayers" is the giveaway. Luke is talking about the worship services at the Temple where, several times a day, every day, all the people who gathered there prayed certain prayers together—again, as we did with the Lord's Prayer

203

earlier. They were dedicated to worship (not just *attending* worship—but attending *to* worship). They worshipped together, seriously, joyfully, devotedly, properly, because they understood better than anybody else why God deserved their worship and what kind of God it was they were worshipping.

They were together in the shared life of faith: studying— serving—celebrating the parade of unimaginable wonders that come out of this common Christian community.

Of course, the picture in Acts doesn't tell the whole story. It's an "action shot," as they call it; it catches them doing what they were doing. But it's a little "posed"—not completely candid.

The picture in Acts 2 doesn't show the struggles and the stumbles along the way. These church people were saved, after all. They had to be; they weren't perfect—any more than we are. The "perfect" part comes later—for them and us.[234]

For now, it's enough to want to be together, and to be focused on learning what the Bible tells us, praying together, breaking bread together—and meeting the needs of all with the resources God has given to each.

Now you know what those first Christians—your ancestors in the faith—devoted themselves to: *"All who believed were together...."* Remember, they weren't the church because they were qualified. They were the church because they were un-qualified—and had the good sense—or the grace of God—to realize it and do something about it—like believing in Jesus.

They devoted themselves to study, fellowship, communion and worship.

What shall we devote ourselves to?

They believed in Jesus and became the church.

You believe in Jesus.

Now what?

෧∙ை

---

[234] 1 Corinthians 13:10; Philippians 3:12.

## Acts 9:1-22 ESV

¹ *But Saul, still breathing threats and murder against the disciples of the Lord, went to the high priest* ² *and asked him for letters to the synagogues at Damascus, so that if he found any belonging to the Way, men or women, he might bring them bound to Jerusalem.* ³ *Now as he went on his way, he approached Damascus, and suddenly a light from heaven shone around him.* ⁴ *And falling to the ground, he heard a voice saying to him, "Saul, Saul, why are you persecuting me?"* ⁵ *And he said, "Who are you, Lord?" And he said, "I am Jesus, whom you are persecuting.* ⁶ *But rise and enter the city, and you will be told what you are to do."* ⁷ *The men who were traveling with him stood speechless, hearing the voice but seeing no one.* ⁸ *Saul rose from the ground, and although his eyes were opened, he saw nothing. So they led him by the hand and brought him into Damascus.* ⁹ *And for three days he was without sight, and neither ate nor drank.*

¹⁰ *Now there was a disciple at Damascus named Ananias. The Lord said to him in a vision, "Ananias." And he said, "Here I am, Lord."* ¹¹ *And the Lord said to him, "Rise and go to the street called Straight, and at the house of Judas look for a man of Tarsus named Saul, for behold, he is praying,* ¹² *and he has seen in a vision a man named Ananias come in and lay his hands on him so that he might regain his sight."* ¹³ *But Ananias answered, "Lord, I have heard from many about this man, how much evil he has done to your saints at Jerusalem.* ¹⁴ *And here he has authority from the chief priests to bind all who call on your name."* ¹⁵ *But the Lord said to him, "Go, for he is a chosen instrument of mine to carry my name before the Gentiles and kings and the children of Israel.* ¹⁶ *For I will show him how much he must suffer for the sake of my name."* ¹⁷ *So Ananias departed and entered the house. And laying his hands on him he said, "Brother Saul, the Lord Jesus who appeared to you on the road by which you came has sent me so that you may regain your sight and be filled with the Holy Spirit."* ¹⁸ *And immediately something like scales fell from his eyes, and he regained his sight. Then he rose and was baptized;* ¹⁹ *and taking food, he was strengthened.*

*For some days he was with the disciples at Damascus.* ²⁰ *And immediately he proclaimed Jesus in the synagogues, saying, "He is the Son of God."* ²¹ *And all who heard him were amazed and said, "Is not this the man who made havoc in Jerusalem of those who called upon this name? And has he not come here for this purpose, to bring them bound before the chief priests?"* [22] *But Saul increased all the more in strength, and confounded the Jews who lived in Damascus by proving that Jesus was the Christ.*

❧❧

# 31.

# Conversion

## Acts 9:1-22 ESV

His goal was to wipe out this weird, new fad that had popped up like a weed in Judaism—this belief that the condemned and crucified criminal Jesus of Nazareth was the Messiah of God. He was determined to rip this heresy out of existence the way you yank crabgrass out of your garden. He was like that policeman in *Les Misérables* [235] who was going to hound the hero and all the other good people in the story to their graves—all in the name of "justice."

And then, like the policeman in the story, he was converted.

One day, he was the most ardent enemy of Christianity. And almost overnight, he became the Apostle Paul, the most influential follower of Christ the world has ever known. And for 30-some years, from that day on the road to Damascus until the day that he, himself, was condemned and executed as a criminal for Christ, this Paul did all in his power—all in the power God gave him—to see that the gospel of Jesus Christ spread like a weed throughout the

---

[235] Victor Hugo, *Les Misérables*, 1862. The obsessive policeman is Inspector Javert, who finally acknowledges the fundamental injustice of the criminal justice system to which he has devoted his life.

world—and flowered in the hearts of the faithful wherever he was able to plant it.

That you are here today—and that you know what you do about Christianity—is due in large measure—directly or indirectly—to Paul. And here today, there is still much that you can learn about your Lord—and your faith—and yourself—from the experience of this man who met the Messiah a few miles outside Damascus.

ॐ

When Paul was persecuting Christians in Jerusalem, he thought he was one of the good guys. When he set off for the Syrian capital to root out Christianity there, he was convinced that he was doing God's will.

One of the reasons it is so hard for people to be converted is that many people just don't see the need. Even among religious people—as Paul certainly believed himself to be (before he "saw the Light")—it is very unusual to consider the possibility that something you say or do or think could be wrong—could be displeasing to God. That's why, most of the time, for God to convert you, He has to interrupt the "regularly scheduled program" of your life for what turns out to be a "special, *spiritual*, news bulletin."

Paul didn't expect to be interrupted in the performance of his self-assigned duties. He was after Christians because if what they preached was right, everything he believed was wrong.

It was easier to believe that he was right and they were wrong. And if he could put them out of business, he would prove—to his satisfaction, anyway—that he had been right all along.

Good plan, *if* you are right.

ॐ

But Jesus decides to join Paul on the road to Damascus to tell him he *isn't* right. Jesus turns on the supernatural spotlights and cranks up the cosmic PA system and points it all right at Paul. Jesus calls him by his Jewish name, Saul. But whatever name He uses, the message is unmistakable: *"Why are you persecuting me?"*

It's an odd way of putting the question—until you remember that Jesus told those who thought they were the good guys but weren't: *"...as you did it to one of the least of these my brothers, you did it to me."*[236]

*Oops!*

❧

Conversion begins with facing up to the truth about yourself—*God's* truth, not yours.

And when you are finally forced to face the truth, it can and should bring you to your knees—just like it did Paul.

Of course, there's always the urge to try to wiggle out of the glare of God's spiritual spotlight.

Jesus asked Paul, *"Why...?"*

Paul responded with his own question: "Who? *Who are you...?"* (Like, who *else* have you been persecuting lately?)

Jesus answered Paul's question: *"I am Jesus...,"* which is scary enough, when you're convinced He's dead. But then Jesus adds, *"...whom you are persecuting...,"* which effectively eliminates all wiggle room for avoiding what is now, unarguably, the truth.

Conversion involves a crisis where you are confronted with the truth about your relationship with Jesus—by Jesus Himself. Jesus asked Paul, *"Why?"* And even though Paul didn't answer His question, Jesus didn't pursue it. Jesus knew the answer already—and He knew that neither Paul's answer, nor any other answer, was acceptable. He asked Paul the question so that Paul could see the truth of that fact for himself.

Conversion requires that you recognize that you are simply out of acceptable options when it comes to what you're going to do

---

[236] Matthew 25:40, ESV.

about God. There is only one acceptable option—to God. And oddly enough—amazingly enough—that one acceptable option to God is not that you "get what's coming to you."

Paul's option for Christians may have been, "Die, heretic!" But that wasn't Christ's option for Paul, or for anyone else.

ঔ৽৽ঙ

*"Rise, and enter the city, and you will be told what you are to do."*
Conversion is where Jesus knocks you down and then lifts you up—the same person, and yet a different person.

*"Enter the city."* Get on with your life—even if it's a whole new life—and even if, at first, somebody else has got to lead you every step of the way.

Conversion means that Somebody else will be telling you what to do from now on. You're no longer in charge of "you." There is something that you are to do—and you will be told what that something is. But until you are told, get up and go about the business you've already been given.

But, of course, the business of conversion is not a one-man operation. Jesus confronts you, knocks you down, lifts you up and then starts mobilizing an army of assistants to help transform you—assistants like Ananias.

Did you notice how similar the instructions were that Jesus gave Paul to what He then gave Ananias: "Get up and go, and here's what you are to do."

And then Jesus goes on, "Go help Paul—this brand-new convert. I 'zapped' him—appeared in person to him—three days ago and he hasn't been able to eat or drink or even see ever since. The only thing I've let him 'see' is a vision of you coming to restore his physical sight."

ঔ৽৽ঙ

When you are converted, Jesus sends other people to touch you and strengthen you and heal you and show you how to be filled with the Holy Spirit. Not perfect people—not spiritual giants—just people who, like you, have been converted and are doing what Jesus has told them to do—even if it terrifies them to do it—as it apparently does Ananias.

Ananias will go and call Paul "Brother"—even though he knows that up until three days before, Paul was anything but his brother. Ananias will treat Paul as his brother because Jesus has told Ananias that Paul is the "vessel" Jesus has chosen for doing the opposite of what Paul had thought God wanted him to do. Paul is the vessel chosen by Jesus to carry the Name of Jesus like Living Water to a world of people quite literally dying for want of it.

It is easy enough for us to see now that Paul was divinely chosen to share the gospel of salvation with the world. It was probably not as clear to Ananias—or to Paul himself—while Paul was persecuting Christians, or when Jesus caught up with him on the Damascus Road, or even while he waited the return of his appetite and his ability to see the world around him.

❧

But the secret of conversion is that Jesus is confronting you in your opposition to Him in order to change you from what you've made of your life to what He's had planned for it all along. Conversion is the beginning of the process of becoming—by God's grace—the person you were always supposed to be.

In the process of his conversion, Paul saw things he never expected to see—such as the light of Christ and the error of his ways. In the process of his conversion, he lost his ability to see what he had been used to seeing. And then, with the help of other Christians and the Holy Spirit, the scales fell from his eyes and he started seeing things in a way that he had never seen them before. Paul started seeing things that only the converted can see.

And in the company of other Christians, he was strengthened. New Savior, new vision, new power.

And new purpose.

Immediately, it says, Paul began proclaiming Jesus. He would spend years figuring out all the theology of Christianity. He would spend his life pounding out its practical application for individual believers and the churches they formed. But it didn't take him any time at all to start telling people what he had seen and heard. He knew what had happened to him.

The evidence of the conversion of Paul was stunning—to the Christians in Damascus like Ananias—to the opponents of Christianity in the synagogue there—and if Paul's own description of his conversion in His letter to the Galatians[237] is any indication—to Paul himself.

Conversion confounds people. You confound people by becoming somebody different from the person you have always been. You confound people who have not been converted because they have not seen what you have seen and cannot understand why you would want to become someone different. You confound other people who have been converted because they—we—never get used to the miracle of conversion because conversion is always a miracle because it only comes through an encounter with Christ.

And your conversion will confound you yourself in the most wonderful way as you realize that the confrontation of your sin is not the end of all hope but its beginning—that the conforming of your life and your heart to Christ is not the forfeiting of your freedom but its firm foundation—that coming into the fellowship of the family of faith is not the way of weakness, but the only way to true power, purpose and love.

ॐ•ॐ

In *Les Misérables*, the policeman bent on persecuting the innocent was not "converted" until the end of the story and the end of his life, though he had been given many opportunities to be

---

[237] Galatians 1:13-24, 2:20.

converted along the way and had rejected them. He lived his whole life as the champion of "the law"—and the enemy of God.

Thank God, the Apostle Paul was different, coming to his senses as a young man when he was called to conversion on the Damascus Road.

With conversion, it's "better late than never," but better still, by far, is "sooner rather than later."

In fact, best of all, is to realize that

"*Today* is the day;
*now* is the time."[238]

&-&

---

[238] 2 Corinthians 6:2.

## Acts 16:9-15 NRSV

*[9] During the night Paul had a vision: there stood a man of Macedonia pleading with him and saying, "Come over to Macedonia and help us." [10] When he had seen the vision, we immediately tried to cross over to Macedonia, being convinced that God had called us to proclaim the good news to them.*

*[11] We set sail from Troas and took a straight course to Samothrace, the following day to Neapolis, [12] and from there to Philippi, which is a leading city of the district of Macedonia and a Roman colony. We remained in this city for some days. [13] On the sabbath day we went outside the gate by the river, where we supposed there was a place of prayer; and we sat down and spoke to the women who had gathered there. [14] A certain woman named Lydia, a worshiper of God, was listening to us; she was from the city of Thyatira and a dealer in purple cloth. The Lord opened her heart to listen eagerly to what was said by Paul. [15] When she and her household were baptized, she urged us, saying, "If you have judged me to be faithful to the Lord, come and stay at my home." And she prevailed upon us.*

ॐ

# 32.

# If You Have Judged Me Faithful

## Acts 16:9-15 NRSV

The scene is a simple one, but not without significance. A small group of women have gathered in a secluded spot by a river. They have gathered to pray to a God they worship. And a smaller group of men come and tell them more about this God to Whom they are praying. Among the men is the Apostle Paul. One of the women is a lady named Lydia.

This Lydia is no ordinary woman, even before she meets Paul and the Master he proclaims. She is a business woman a manufacturer and a merchant. She is a dealer in purple cloth, the most expensive material there is. She is a woman of wealth and status and sophistication. She is, as the Romans would put it, a *mater-familias*—the mother of the family—the female head of a household.

Lydia hears the good news of Jesus Christ and believes it. She shares this good news with those who live in her house and under her authority, and they receive the salvation of Jesus as well.

They are all baptized. And now she wants to *know* one thing and *do* one thing. She wants to know if Paul and the other missionaries have judged her faithful to Jesus. And what she wants to do is to bring the church into her home. And in this, she is a worthy subject for our consideration on this day we devote to mothers.

We praise our mothers and honor their sacrifices and accomplishments. God bless you mothers who are here among us today. But there is a sense in which every woman is to be a mother—a spiritual *materfamilias*—to those in the family of Jesus Christ.

Look at Lydia. She is determined to bring her faith into her home. She is determined to become the spiritual leader of those who depend on her. Every Christian woman is to live so that she— you—can be judged faithful to the Lord, and you are to express that faithfulness in ways that will bring the church of Jesus Christ home to those who are part of your functional household, however large or small that may have become.

Lydia creates a church in her home by inviting Paul and Silas and the others into her home and making it the staging ground for their outreach to the people around her.

Later, she will draw other believers into her home. It says later in this chapter that after God frees Paul and Silas from prison, they go to Lydia's house to see the brothers and sisters gathered there— to see the church in Lydia's home.

We are now a thousand strong, here at this church. No one's house will hold us. And you may have downsized from a large house to a small apartment or even to a room. You may be living alone.

But wherever you live, you can bring the church of Jesus Christ home with you. You can be faithful to Him and, in that faithfulness, create an environment that draws the people you encounter—wherever you may be—into an awareness of the presence and power of God.

Ladies, you can be a spiritual mother to anyone through your faithfulness to Christ and your determination to make the place you live a place where the Holy Spirit is at home.

Lydia was the first convert Paul won to Christ in Philippi—the first new Christian in the region of Macedonia. Lydia was the first person to become a believer in Greece, and therefore, in Europe.

But the greater significance is that she was judged faithful to the gospel—that she made a place for Jesus in her heart and her life. She made a place for Jesus and His Church in her home and in her world. Lydia's faithfulness made her a spiritual mother to a handful in her home—and to a multitude of believers, a numberless spiritual family who would grow out of her house and her heart.

Thank God for our mothers. Thank God for the spiritual mothers who nurture God's family in faithfulness.

৵৽

# Indices

## Sermon Titles in Alphabetical Order

## *Sermon Titles in Alphabetical Order*

## Sermon Texts in Biblical Order

# Sermon Texts in Biblical Order

## *Additional Scripture Passages Referenced*

# Additional Scripture Passages Referenced

## Additional Scripture Passages Referenced

# Additional Scripture Passages Referenced

## Additional Scripture Passages Referenced

## Additional Scripture Passages Referenced

## Additional Scripture Passages Referenced

# Additional Scripture Passages Referenced

## Sermon Texts in Lectionary Order

## Sermon Texts in Lectionary Order

## Sermons from Luke and Acts in Other Volumes